my revision notes

WJEC and Eduqas GCSE

COMPUTER SCIENCE

Ian Paget and Robert Wicks

HODDER
EDUCATION
AN HACHETTE UK COMPANY

The Publishers would like to thank the following for permission to reproduce copyright material.

Photo credits
P.42 (left) taken from Greenfoot software, **(right)** Copyright 1991-1995 by Stichting Mathematisch Centrum, Amsterdam, The Netherlands; **p.61** © NASA Photo/Alamy Stock Photo; **p.80** taken from Greenfoot software.

Acknowledgements
Every effort has been made to trace all copyright holders, but if any have been inadvertently overlooked, the Publishers will be pleased to make the necessary arrangements at the first opportunity.

Although every effort has been made to ensure that website addresses are correct at time of going to press, Hodder Education cannot be held responsible for the content of any website mentioned in this book. It is sometimes possible to find a relocated web page by typing in the address of the home page for a website in the URL window of your browser.

Hachette UK's policy is to use papers that are natural, renewable and recyclable products and made from wood grown in well-managed forests and other controlled sources. The logging and manufacturing processes are expected to conform to the environmental regulations of the country of origin.

Orders: please contact Hachette UK Distribution, Hely Hutchinson Centre, Milton Road, Didcot, Oxfordshire, OX11 7HH. Telephone: +44 (0)1235 827827. Email education@hachette.co.uk Lines are open from 9 a.m. to 5 p.m., Monday to Friday. You can also order through our website: www.hoddereducation.co.uk.

ISBN: 978 1 5104 5493 4

First published in 2018 by
Hodder Education,
An Hachette UK Company
Carmelite House
50 Victoria Embankment
London EC4Y 0DZ
www.hoddereducation.co.uk

Impression number 10 9 8 7 6 5 4

Year   2023 2022

Cover photo © 2017 Andrew Ostrovsky

Typeset in Bembo Std Regular 11/13pt by Aptara Inc.

Printed by CPI Group (UK) Ltd, Croydon CR0 4YY

A catalogue record for this title is available from the British Library.

Get the most from this book

Everyone has to decide his or her own revision strategy, but it is essential to review your work, learn it and test your understanding. These Revision Notes will help you to do that in a planned way, topic by topic. Use this book as the cornerstone of your revision and don't hesitate to write in it — personalise your notes and check your progress by ticking off each section as you revise.

Tick to track your progress

Use the revision planner on pages iv, v and vi to plan your revision, topic by topic. Tick each box when you have

- revised and understood a topic
- tested yourself
- practised the exam questions and gone online to check your answers and complete the quick quizzes

You can also keep track of your revision by ticking off each topic heading in the book. You may find it helpful to add your own notes as you work through each topic.

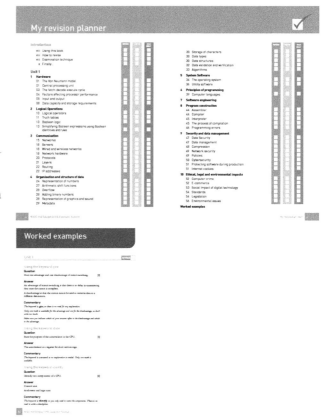

Features to help you succeed

Key terms

A number of key terms are used and defined for you as you work through this guide. Make sure you learn them so that you can use the terms accurately and precisely in the exams in order to gain top marks. A glossary of programming terms can be found on page 96 whilst the full glossary can be found at **www.hoddereducation.co.uk/ myrevisionnotesdownloads.**

Exam tips

Exam tips are given throughout the book to help you polish your exam technique in order to maximise your chances in the exam.

Now test yourself

These short, knowledge-based questions are the first step in testing your learning. Answers are available online.

My revision planner

Introduction

REVISED   TESTED   EXAM READY

Unit 1

1   Hardware

2   Logical Operations

3   Communication

4   Organisation and structure of data

Unit 2

REVISED TESTED EXAM READY

Countdown to my exams

6–8 weeks to go

- Start by looking at the specification — make sure you know exactly what material you need to revise and the style of the examination. Use the revision planner on pages iv, v and vi to familiarise yourself with the topics.
- Organise your notes, making sure you have covered everything on the specification. The revision planner will help you to group your notes into topics.
- Work out a realistic revision plan that will allow you time for relaxation. Set aside days and times for all the subjects that you need to study, and stick to your timetable.
- Set yourself sensible targets. Break your revision down into focused sessions of around 40 minutes, divided by breaks. These Revision Notes organise the basic facts into short, memorable sections to make revising easier.

REVISED ☐

2–6 weeks to go

- Read through the relevant sections of this book and refer to the exam tips, exam summaries, typical mistakes and key terms. Tick off the topics as you feel confident about them. Highlight those topics you find difficult and look at them again in detail.
- Test your understanding of each topic by working through the 'Now test yourself' questions in the book. Look up the answers at the back of the book.
- Make a note of any problem areas as you revise, and ask your teacher to go over these in class.
- Look at past papers. They are one of the best ways to revise and practise your exam skills. Write or prepare planned answers to the exam practice questions provided in this book.
- Use the revision activities to try out different revision methods. For example, you can make notes using mind maps, spider diagrams or flash cards.
- Track your progress using the revision planner and give yourself a reward when you have achieved your target.

REVISED ☐

One week to go

- Try to fit in at least one more timed practice of an entire past paper and seek feedback from your teacher, comparing your work closely with the mark scheme.
- Check the revision planner to make sure you haven't missed out any topics. Brush up on any areas of difficulty by talking them over with a friend or getting help from your teacher.
- Attend any revision classes put on by your teacher. Remember, he or she is an expert at preparing people for examinations.

REVISED ☐

The day before the examination

- Flick through these Revision Notes for useful reminders, for example the exam tips, exam summaries, typical mistakes and key terms.
- Check the time and place of your examination.
- Make sure you have everything you need — extra pens and pencils, tissues, a watch, bottled water, sweets.
- Allow some time to relax and have an early night to ensure you are fresh and alert for the examinations.

REVISED ☐

My exams

GCSE Computer Science Unit 1

Date:..

Time: ....

Location: ....

GCSE Computer Science Unit 2

Date:..

Time: ....

Location: ....

Introduction

Using this book

You can use this book to revise for WJEC GCSE in Computer Science.

● This is a **revision** book.
● It does not attempt to delve deeply into any of the topics.
● You should study individual sections using other available text books, lesson notes, attending classes and so on.
● It is to remind you of the essential vocabulary needed.
● It gives summaries of advantages and disadvantages of various computer science systems and practices.

This book is to be used **after** you have studied the subject.

The book is divided into Unit 1 and Unit 2 covering the topics in the specification. Answers for the 'Now test yourself' questions as well as a glossary listing key terms can be found online at www.hoddereducation.co.uk/myrevisionnotesdownloads.

Unit 1

REVISED

● Understanding Computer Science
● Written examination: 1 hour 45 minutes
● 50% of the qualification
● 100 marks

Unit 2

REVISED

● Computational Thinking and Programming
● On-screen examination: 2 hours
● 30% of the qualification
● 60 marks

How to revise

REVISED

Revision is an **active** undertaking. You cannot revise successfully using reading skills alone. There are several ways of making sure that the content you are revising stays in your long-term memory.

● After you have read a section put the book down and summarise the essential points in writing.
● Use past examination questions and answer them. Always check on the kind of answers the examiners are looking for.
● Revise with a friend or get a member of the family to test you.
● Revise at a desk or table, not lying in bed!

Examination technique

REVISED

The first and foremost technique is to **be prepared**. The examination is not a magic wand that will fill your head with answers on the day of the exam. It is a test of what you have learned in the past year or two years. If you are properly prepared you will more easily relax.

Be fully aware of the nature of the exam paper before you go into the exam room. You should have tried several 'mock' papers and have a good idea of the format of the examination, how many questions to expect, whether there are any choices and so on.

It is important to look out for the signs in all questions for what the examiner requires. These will be such things as the **key words**.

- Give
- State
- Identify
- Describe
- Explain
- Compare
- Contrast
- Discuss

Look out for
- the **number of lines** to be filled in
- the **number of marks** to be awarded.

Once you have answered a question read through your answer and try to see where the examiner could have given you marks. Have you done enough? Remember that repeating the words in the question as part of the answer will never gain marks. You must gain each mark with a new expression to show that you know what you are writing about.

Very briefly the key words will require the following responses. (*Though keep your wits about you as there are no hard and fast rules here.*)

Give, **State**, or **Identify** will just need a word, phrase or sentence and will usually be worth one mark.

Describe will require at least a sentence. (Look at the marks available to know how many points to make.)

Compare/Contrast will mean that you need to identify a factor common to two systems and describe that factor for each.

Explain will probably require a description of how or why something is done and then perhaps an advantage or disadvantage or some other factor described.

Discuss is the highest order of question.

You will need to cover
- the advantages and disadvantages of something and,
- make points and expand them to finally reach a conclusion.

There may be other key words used by the examiners, but they will probably have similar meanings to the above. The main things to be aware of when answering questions are
- What is examiner trying to get me to write?
- Which part of the specification is being examined?

If you finish early don't colour in all the round letters on the front of the examination paper. That gives the wrong impression to an examiner. Go over your questions and check that where there are say four marks, you have given an answer where the examiner can put four ticks. If it is a discussion question, have you really explained yourself well?

Introduction

Remember working at a revision text is an **active** task. It is not just about reading, but about remembering and associating facts learned in this book with facts learned elsewhere. Definitions and descriptions, advantages and disadvantages must be learned, just as you would have to learn a poem, the dialogue of a play or a piece of music. In addition to the learning of facts there needs to be understanding so these facts can be fitted to different scenarios. Revising is hard work but, in the end, very rewarding. If you can go into the examination room, open your paper and see computer science terms with which you are familiar and questions you can answer with confidence, you will feel well rewarded for your efforts.

Good luck with your revision and your examinations. We hope you find this book useful.

1 Hardware

Computer hardware consists of the physical parts of the computer, including
- **central processing unit (CPU)**
- **soundcard**
- **motherboard**
- **graphics processing unit (GPU)**
- **input** and **output units**
- **storage** units (primary and secondary).

The internal organisational structure of a computer is known as the **computer architecture**. There are many designs, including the
- **Von Neumann** model
- **Harvard** model.

The Von Neumann model

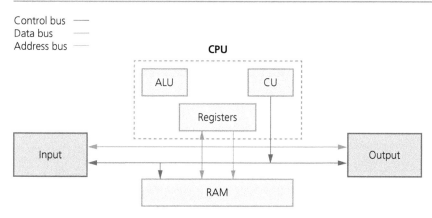

Control bus ——
Data bus ——
Address bus ——

Figure 1.1.1 The Von Neumann model

Central processing unit (CPU)

The **central processing unit** consists of the components of the computer that process the instructions. These instructions may be
- simple arithmetic
- logical operations.

There is a CPU at the heart of every computer. It is regarded as the 'brain' of the computer. The main CPU architecture used today is the Von Neumann architecture.

Every program instruction is interpreted and executed within the CPU. To process the data a computer must have facilities to
- input instructions and data
- store the data and program instructions (a memory)
- output the results of the processing
- control and interpret the machine language and send appropriate signals to each of the other components.

Components of the CPU

- Control unit (CU)
- Arithmetic and logic unit (ALU)
- Registers
- Buses
- Internal memory

The control unit

- Supervises the **fetch–decode–execute cycle.**
- Sends and receives signals from all parts of the computer.
- Decodes instructions in the current instruction register (CIR).
- Selects machine resources.
- Selects the particular mathematical operation to be used.
- Ensures that all processes take place at the right time and in the correct order.

The arithmetic and logic unit

- Processes and manipulates data.
- Carries out simple arithmetic operations, such as addition and subtraction.
- Carries out logical operations, such as comparing two values.

The registers

The CU needs somewhere to store details of the operations being dealt with by the fetch–decode–execute cycle. The ALU needs somewhere to put the results of any operations it carries out. These are called **registers** and, although they have limited storage capacity, they play a vital role in the operation of the computer. Registers are usually much faster to access than internal memory since they must be accessed so often.

Registers that are used by the processor as part of the fetch–execute cycle include the

- **current instruction register** (CIR) that stores the instruction that is currently being executed by the processor
- **program counter** (PC) that stores the memory location of the next instruction that will be needed by the processor
- **memory address register** (MAR) that stores the memory location where data is currently being written to or read from
- **accumulator** (ACC) that stores the results of calculations made by the ALU.

> **Exam tip**
>
> A register is a temporary, fast access storage location found in the CPU where data or control information is temporarily stored.

Buses

Buses are pathways using groups of parallel wires that connect the processor to the various input and output controllers being used by the computer. They are also used to connect the internal components of the CPU, known as registers, and to connect the CPU to memory. They are the

- data bus
- address bus
- control bus.

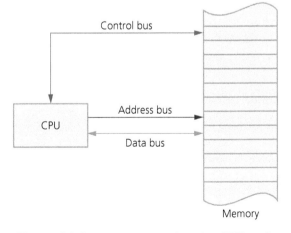

Figure 1.1.2 Buses connecting the CPU to the memory

The data bus
- carries instructions and data between the processor and memory as the program is run
- transfers the data both to and from memory
- moves the data to and from the I/O controllers.

The address bus
- only carries data in one direction – from the processor into memory
- is used by the processor and carries the memory address of the next instruction or data item
- is used to access anything that is stored in memory, not just instructions, to the processor.

The control bus
- is used by the CPU to communicate with other units in the computer
- ensures that the control information reaches the right place at the right time
- usually only sends data one-way.

Internal memory
- Memory built into the computer such as
  - random access memory (RAM)
  - read only memory (ROM)
  - registers.
- Fast access memory is directly accessed by the processor.

Check your understanding
REVISED

1 Write down **five** items of hardware.
2 Name **two** different types of computer architecture.
3 Give the full name to these registers:

CIR	
MAR	
ACC	
PC	

The fetch-decode-execute cycle
REVISED

There are three steps to processing instructions given by a currently running program:
1 **The fetch cycle**
   - The PC holds the address of the next instruction to be executed.
   - A copy of the address in the PC is sent to the MAR.
   - The processor uses this address to find the instruction in the memory.
   - The contents of the data in that memory location are sent to the CIR.
   - The PC moves on one to point at the next instruction to be carried out.
   - The cycle is repeated until all instructions have been carried out.
2 **Decode**
   - The CU checks the instruction in the CIR.
   - The instruction is decoded to determine the action that needs to be carried out.

3 Execute

○ The processor carries out the instruction.
○ The next instruction is fetched.

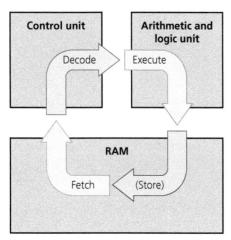

Figure 1.1.3 Fetch-decode-execute cycle

Factors affecting processor performance

Cache memory

- Fast access temporary storage on the CPU.
- Used to store instructions and data that are needed frequently.
- Most commonly used functions or data used in a program are placed into the cache.

Cache memory has the disadvantage of being more expensive than random access memory (RAM), but the advantage is that the cache can be accessed much more quickly than main memory, so programs run faster.

Clock speed

- Indicates how fast each instruction will be executed.
- Increasing the clock speed should increase the speed at which the processor executes instructions.

Multiple cores

A **core** contains an ALU, CU and registers. Multiple processors can be incorporated onto a single chip to make a multi-core processor. A dual-core processor, therefore, has two cores on one chip and will run much faster than a single-core system.

- In a single-core CPU, each instruction is processed one after the other.
- In a dual-core CPU, two instructions may be processed at the same time, meaning the instructions should be processed twice as fast as a single core.
- Faster speeds, in theory, can be gained using four cores (quad cores) or more.

Performance may be affected by one core waiting for the result of another and, therefore, cannot carry out any more instructions, leading to the performance being no better than a single-core processor.

Multiple cores increase the processor cost, though this is offset by the increase in processing speed.

> **Exam tip**
>
> Factors affecting speed should be considered as a whole rather than choosing one aspect to fix the problem. There is no point fitting a faster clock to a computer if you do not change the components that are going to make good use of the clock pulse.

Processor instruction sets

An **instruction set** is the complete set of all the instructions in machine code that can be recognised and executed by a CPU. The instruction sets are libraries of all the things the processor can be asked to do.

Computers may be classed as
● reduced instruction set computer (RISC)
● complex instruction set computer (CISC).

Reduced instruction set computer

RISC processors can process a limited number of relatively simple instructions.

The advantages of a RISC processor are
● it can process these simpler instructions quickly
● processing simpler instructions requires less circuitry for decoding and executing
● less power consumption
● less heat being generated.

Complex instruction set computer

CISC processors can process a large number of complex instructions.

An advantage of a CISC processor is
● the complex instructions can be processed without having to break them down into many simpler instructions.

The disadvantages of a CISC processor is
● it requires large amounts of circuitry to decode and execute the instructions (so the CPUs are larger)
● more power consumption needed
● more heat being generated.

> **Exam tip**
>
> Because RISC chips produce less heat and consume less power than CISC, they are ideal for use in mobile phones.

Check your understanding

REVISED

1 Draw a simple diagram to explain the fetch-decode-execute cycle.
2 Explain the difference between RISC and CISC.
3 Name **three** factors that are likely to affect the speed of a computer.

Input and output

REVISED

Input devices

An input device allows data – such as text, images, video or sound – to be entered into a computer system.

Input device	Example of use
Keyboard	Typing in text
Scanner	Scanning documents or pictures
Mouse, roller ball, touch pad	Moving a cursor on screen
Sip-puff tube, foot mouse, eye-typer	Alternative for someone who cannot use a mouse
Microphone	Voice input

Output devices

An output device can be used to produce printed documents, on-screen data and sound.

Output device	Example of use
Printer	Printing documents
Monitor	Displaying the output on screen
Speaker	Producing sounds from the computer

Primary storage

Random access memory (RAM)

- Used for the temporary storage of currently running programs and data.
- Consists of a large number of storage locations each of which is identified by a unique address.
- Data in each storage location can be changed.
- It is volatile so data is lost when the power is switched off.

For example, when you are working on a word-processed document, the program you are using and the data within the document are both stored in RAM.

Read-only memory (ROM)

- Used for the permanent storage of data.
- The data in each storage location cannot be changed.
- Non-volatile so data is not lost when the power is switched off.

Flash memory

- Used for the permanent storage of data.
- The data stored in flash memory can be changed.
- Flash memory is permanent – data is not lost when the power is switched off.

RAM Cache memory

- Used for the temporary storage of frequently accessed data and instructions.
- Consists of a small number of store locations that can be accessed very quickly by the CPU.
- Quicker than RAM.
- Cache memory is volatile.

> **Exam tip**
>
> Both ROM and flash memory can be used for storing programs such as the BIOS. The disadvantage of using ROM to store the BIOS is that it cannot be upgraded, but with flash memory it can.

Summary of different types of memory

	Volatile	Permanent	Editable	Relative Speed
RAM	Yes	No	Yes	**
ROM	No	Yes	No	***
Flash memory	No	Yes	Yes	*
Cache memory	Yes	No	Yes	****

Secondary storage

Secondary storage is non-volatile. It is known as backing store. When the computer is switched off, the data stored here is not lost. It is used for storing things such as

- applications such as a word processor
- saved programs
- games
- images.

Different types of backing storage are shown in this table.

Media	Use	Relative durability	Portable	Relative speed
Magnetic disc (internal hard drive)	Storing files permanently in the computer	*	No	***
External magnetic disc	Backing up work	*	Yes	***
Magnetic tape	Backing up large amounts of work commercially	*	Yes	*
Optical disc CD, DVD, Blu-ray	Storing multimedia files	***	Yes	**
Flash disc	Transporting data from home to school	****	Yes	****
Secure Digital Card (SD)	In cameras	****	Yes	****

Check your understanding

1 Fill in the blanks in this table.

Device	Reason
	Typing into a computer
Scanner	
	Useful for someone who cannot move their arms
Microphone	

2 Tick the appropriate box to show whether the following are input or output devices.

Device	Input	Output
Keyboard		
Scanner		
Foot mouse		
Printer		
Roller ball		
Monitor		

3 Which of the following is volatile memory?

a) RAM,   b) ROM,   c) Flash memory

Data capacity and storage requirements

Data capacity is the amount of data a storage device can hold.

The smallest unit of data is that used by a switch. A switch can be on or off and can be represented by 1 bit.

Switch State	Bit
On	1
Off	0

Data units

Unit	Symbol	Value
Bit	b	1 bit
Nibble	–	4 bits
Byte	B	8 bits
Kilobyte	KB	1024 B
Megabyte	MB	1024 KB
Gigabyte	GB	1024 MB
Terabyte	TB	1024 GB
Petabyte	PB	1024 TB
Exabyte	EB	1024 PB
Zettabyte	ZB	1024 EB
Yottabyte	YB	1024 ZB

Capacity	Typical use	Number of 0s and 1s
1 B	Single letter or number 0 to 255	8
1 KB	Short email without images	8 192
1 MB	1 minute of music stored as an MP3	8 388 608
700 MB	Maximum amount of data that can be stored on a CD-ROM	5 872 025 600

Additional hardware components

These components are required to complete the computer architecture.

Motherboard

The **motherboard** is the circuit board to which all the components of the computer are connected. Buses take the data from one part of the mother board to another. The CPU is fixed into the motherboard.

Graphics processor unit

The **graphics processor unit** (GPU) is a specialised chip and circuit board which helps processing when applications are using 3D graphics and video animation. The GPU renders the images, animations and video for the computer screen. It helps make the images appearing on screen faster and smoother to give the best experience in games and movies.

Soundcard

- Takes sound input from a microphone or other source as analogue data and converts it into digital data to be processed by the computer.
- Converts digital data stored in the computer into analogue form to be used as audio output.

Embedded systems

An **embedded system** is a combination of software and hardware created for a specific purpose. A PC is a general-purpose machine designed to carry out multiple tasks. Embedded systems are made for a specific use and are often mass produced. They consist of a program on ROM or flash disc running a simple machine.

Examples where embedded systems are used are
- washing machines
- microwave ovens
- automatic garage doors
- motor car engines using sensor input.

Check your understanding
REVISED

1 How many bytes make a Kilobyte?
2 How many characters can be represented by one byte?
3 Explain why the graphics processing unit is important.
4 Give an example of the use of an embedded system which is not on the list on this page.

Now test yourself
TESTED

1 Describe the role of the following devices:
   a) Graphics processing unit [2]
   b) Embedded system [2]
2 In a certain system, one byte represents one character.
   a) How many characters can be represented by 2 KB?
      (Show your working.) [2]
   b) i) Explain why a CD-ROM would not be able to store a movie using 8 GB. [2]
      ii) State the storage device that would be needed to store a movie that used 8 GB. [1]

Answers available online

2 Logical operations

Computers function using millions of switches. These can either be in the ON or OFF position, like a light switch, which can be represented by the digits 1 or 0. These two digits can also represent the words True and False.

ON	1	TRUE
OFF	0	FALSE

This means that logical operations carried out by the computer can be represented by 0s and 1s.

Logical operations are useful for
- designing electronic circuits
- computer programming.

Logical operators

There are several rules for combining 0s and 1s. These are known as logical operators. Each rule has a name. The rules cover every possible combination of two bits.

You will need to know the rules for
- **AND**
- **OR**
- **NOT**
- **XOR** (meaning exclusive OR).

> **Exam tip**
>
> To be able to answer any question on logic, you must learn the rules for AND, OR, NOT and XOR. Check you know them now!

Logical operator rules

AND		
IN		OUT
0	0	0
0	1	0
1	0	0
1	1	1

OR		
IN		OUT
0	0	0
0	1	1
1	0	1
1	1	1

NOT	
IN	OUT
0	1
1	0

XOR		
IN		OUT
0	0	0
0	1	1
1	0	1
1	1	0

Examples using the tables above

1 AND 0 = 0

1 OR 0 = 1

NOT 1 = 0

1 XOR 0 = 1

Check your understanding

Complete these expressions.

1 AND 1	=
NOT 0	=
1 XOR 1	=
0 OR 0	=

Truth tables

Truth tables are used to solve logical problems.

When a computer program is made, it is important that the logic circuits in the computer know which output is expected from which inputs.

Imagine a simple human problem. A burglar alarm is set to sound a warning if a window is open. To a person, that sounds simple, but, a computer must be taught the rules.

The alarm could be off or on and the window could be open or closed.

The computer must know all possible combinations. A truth table using AND is required.

Alarm possibilities		
Alarm on	**Window open**	**Result**
NO	NO	No alarm
NO	YES	No alarm
YES	NO	No alarm
YES	YES	Alarm

The truth table shows that the alarm will only sound if the window is open AND the alarm is switched on.

We can change the NO to 0 and the YES to 1.

Figure 1.2.1

The table will then look like this.

Alarm possibilities		
Alarm on	**Window open**	**Result**
0	0	0
0	1	0
1	0	0
1	1	1

Alarm table		
A	**B**	**C**
0	0	0
0	1	0
1	0	0
1	1	1

This can be simplified to

A AND B = C

1 Assume an alarm is set. It will go off if either a window is open or a door is open.
  Complete the tables below.
  Step 1

Alarm possibilities – alarm is on		
Window open	**Door open**	**Result**
NO	NO	
NO		Alarm
YES	NO	
YES		Alarm

Step 2

Alarm possibilities – alarm is on		
Window open	**Door open**	**Result**
	0	
0		1
	0	
1		1

Step 3

Alarm table		
A	**B**	**C**

This can be simplified to
A ___ B = C

2 Complete a truth table for an alarm system where the alarm A is connected to a window B and a door C.
  (Hint: work out A AND B first then OR the result with C.)

Alarm truth table				
A	**B**	**A AND B**	**C**	**D**
0	0		0	
0	0		1	
0	1		0	
0	1		1	
1	0		0	
1	0		1	
1	1		0	
1	1		1	

Boolean logic

Boolean algebra is named after the mathematician George Boole (1815–1864). It is a set of rules that help to solve Boolean expressions.

Logic rules can be combined to give different outputs.

Example

Solve (1 OR 0) AND (NOT 1)

Just as in mathematics, solve the brackets first.

From the tables (1 OR 0) gives 1

From the tables (NOT 1) gives 0

We are now left with

1 AND 0

From the tables you can see that this is 0

So, (1 OR 0) AND (NOT 1) = 0

Writing more complicated expressions would be awkward if we had to keep writing out AND and OR, and so on, in full. So, a shorthand has been developed.

Operator	Symbol	Example
AND	.	A.B
OR	+	A+B
NOT	–	$\overline{A}$

No special symbol for XOR is used in this course.

You will be expected to know and use the entries in the table below to help simplify Boolean expressions.

	AND	OR
Commutative law	A.B = B.A	A+B = B+A
Associative law	(A.B).C = A.(B.C)	(A+B)+C = A+(B+C)
Distributive law	(A+B).C = (A.C)+(B.C)	(A+B)+C = (A+B)+(A+C)
	A.1 = A	A+0 = A
	A.0 = 0	A+1 = 1
	A.$\overline{A}$ = 0	A+$\overline{A}$ = 1
	A.A = A	A+A = A

Simplifying Boolean expressions using Boolean identities and rules

Example 1

Simplify

(A.B) + (B.C)

The table of identities show that A.B is the same as B.A (commutative law).

So, we can write

$(B.A) + (B.C)$

Using the distributive law, the expression becomes

$B.(A+C)$

Thus

$(A.B) + (B.C) = B.(A+C)$

This is read as (A AND B) OR (B AND C) equals B AND (A OR C).

Example 2

Simplify $(A + \bar{A}) + A$

Solve the brackets first, $(A + \bar{A}) = 1$

$1 + A = 1$

Thus $(A + \bar{A}) + A = 1$

Check your understanding

REVISED

1 Using the appropriate symbols, complete the Boolean expression that represents this truth table.

A	B	A.B	B+(A.B)	C
0	0	0	0	1
0	1	0	1	1
1	0	0	0	0
1	1	1	1	1

$C = B + (A.B)$ _____

2 Tick True or False in the following table.

	True	False
A.1 = 1		
$A + \bar{A} = A$		
(X.Y) + (X.Z) = X.(Y+Z)		
1 = A + 0		

Now test yourself

TESTED

1 Fill in the truth table.

A	B	$\bar{A}$	$\bar{A}+B$	B.($\bar{A}+B$)
0	0			
0	1			
1	0			
1	1			

[4]

Use the table to simplify B.($\bar{A}+B$) [1]

2 Simplify (A+B) + (A+C) [1]

3 Draw a truth table for XOR [2]

Answers available online

3 Communication

A **network** is a collection of computing devices connected together.

Advantages of networks
- Hardware can be shared (e.g. several computers can use the same printer).
- Software can be shared (e.g. a number of workstations can all load up the same program from a file server).
- Data can be shared (e.g. a number of computers can access the same database stored on a file server).
- Computers may communicate between each other with messages or email.
- Administration is centralised.
- Users can log into any networked device.

Disadvantages of networks
- Viruses can be spread to all computers on a network.
- Hackers may access computers on a network.
- Can be expensive to install.
- Networks may be slower than using standalone computers.

Types of network

There are two main types of network. They are
- local area network (LAN)
- wide area network (WAN).

A LAN is a network in which the computer systems are all located relatively close to each other, for example, in the same building or on the same site, such as a school.

A WAN is a network in which the computers systems are all located relatively far from each other, for example, in different buildings all over the country or in different countries. The internet is an example of a WAN. Many LANs could be linked using a WAN.

The topology of a network is the way in which the connections of a network are arranged.

Network topologies

Star network

Each node of the network is connected to a central node which may be a computer (file server) or a hub.

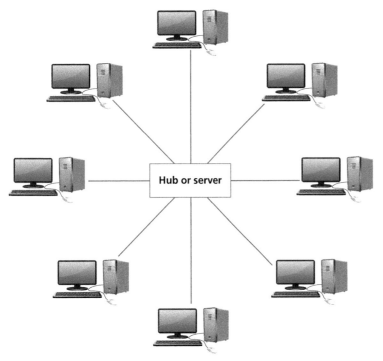

Figure 1.3.1 **Star network topology**

Advantages of a star topology	Disadvantages of a star topology
<ul><li>Faster connection speed as each node has a dedicated cable.</li><li>Will not slow down as much as other network topologies when many users are online.</li><li>Fault-finding is simpler as individual faults are easier to trace.</li><li>Relatively secure as the connection from client to server is unique.</li><li>New nodes can be added without affecting the others.</li></ul>	<ul><li>Expensive to setup due to increased cabling costs.</li><li>If a cable fails, then that node may not be able to receive data.</li><li>Difficult to install as multiple cables are needed; the problem is exaggerated where the LAN is split across a number of buildings.</li><li>The server can get congested as all communications must pass through it.</li></ul>

Ring network

The nodes are connected in a ring. Data is transmitted around the ring, being passed from one node to the next until it arrives at its destination.

Data generally flows in one direction only.

In a token ring network, a node wanting to transmit data waits for a 'token' to come round. The data is attached to this token and sent round the ring. Each node checks the token to see if it is for them. The receiving node downloads the data.

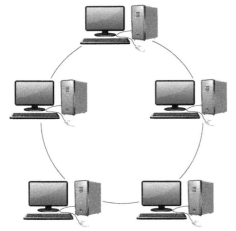

Figure 1.3.2 **Ring network topology**

Advantages of a ring topology	Disadvantages of a ring topology
● Data is quickly transferred without a bottleneck giving consistent data transfer speeds. ● The transmission of data is relatively simple as data travels in one direction only. ● Adding additional nodes has very little impact on bandwidth. ● It prevents network collisions.	● If any of the computer systems fail, the ring is broken and data cannot be transmitted efficiently. ● If there is a problem with the main cable or connection, the entire network goes down. ● It is difficult to troubleshoot the ring. ● Because all nodes are wired together, to add another you must temporarily shut down the network.

Bus network

A cable, known as a bus, carries a message. As the message arrives at each workstation, the workstation checks the destination address contained in the message to see if it matches its own. If the address does not match, the workstation ignores it. If the workstation addresses match those contained in the message, the workstation processes the message.

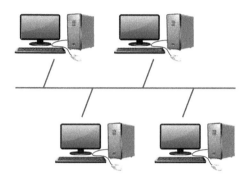

Figure 1.3.3 **Bus network technology**

Advantages of a bus topology	Disadvantages of a bus topology
● Cheaper to install compared to the other network topologies. ● Easy network to install. ● Easy to add new nodes by branching them off the main cable.	● Not that secure, as all data is transmitted down one main cable. ● Transmission times get slower when more users are on the network. ● If the main cable fails, then all clients are affected. ● More difficult to find faults.

Mesh network

A mesh topology uses direct connection between nodes. Every node in the mesh has a connection to every other node. Data can be transferred directly or routed via other nodes.

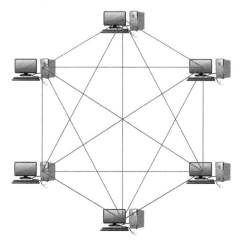

Figure 1.3.4 **Mesh network technology**

Advantages of a mesh topology	Disadvantages of a mesh topology
• A reliable topology for transferring data. • Very robust as there is no single point which, if it fails, will bring down the network.	• Expensive to set up. • Complex to install.

Check your understanding

REVISED

1 Name **three** network topologies.
2 Find out what network topology is used by your school.
3 Name **three** advantages of using networks.

Servers

REVISED

A **file server** is the computer on the network that stores the files used by other workstations. For instance, a large database may be stored on the file server.

A printer may be connected to the bus, or to one of the workstations which can act as a print server. The printer then becomes part of the network.

Wired and wireless networks

REVISED

A wireless network connects devices using radio signals. A wireless device usually connects to a **router** using **access points**.

A wired network uses physical connections, usually **copper cables** or **fibre optic cables**, to connect devices. Copper cables are usually standard twisted pair cables called Category 6 (Cat 6) cables.

Advantages of a wired network	Disadvantages of a wired network
Transmission speeds tend to be faster than a wireless network.	Difficult to install as wires must be routed to every station.
Tend to be more secure than wireless networks.	Expensive to install.

Advantages of a wireless network	Disadvantages of a wireless network
Mobile equipment can easily log into the network.	Can be hacked more easily than wired network.
Easy to install.	Transmission speeds slow as more users join.
Cheap to install.	

Network hardware

REVISED

A number of items of hardware is used in creating both wired and wireless networks.

Hardware	Purpose
Router	Forwards packets of data along a network. Often used where two networks are connected. Determines best path for the packets.
Hub	A connection point between cables in a network.
Switch	Filters and forwards data packets to intended destination.
Bridge	Connects one LAN to another.
Gateway	Connects a LAN to a WAN such as the internet.

Switching

Data can travel around networks in two ways
- circuit switching
- packet switching.

Circuit switching

- Provides a dedicated link between two nodes.
- No other data can be transmitted along the same route while the connection is open.
- A landline telephone system is an example of a circuit switched network.

Advantages of circuit switching	Disadvantages of circuit switching
<ul><li>It is very reliable.</li><li>Once the connection is established, it is fast.</li><li>Tends to be error free.</li></ul>	<ul><li>Takes time to establish a connection.</li><li>Should anywhere on the route fail, then the connection will be broken.</li></ul>

Packet switching

- Data is split up into small packets.
- Each packet carries the address of its destination.
- As the packet arrives at a switch or a router, the address is read and it is sent along the next free path.
- Each packet contains information about how many packets there are in the message.
- Each packet has information explaining where it fits into the message.
- Packets may arrive at the destination in a different order to which they were sent, but can reassemble using the information contained in the packet once all packets have arrived.

The source address	The destination address
Information which enables the data to be reassembled into its original form	
Other tracking information	
The data itself	A checksum that checks that the data has not been corrupted

Figure 1.3.5 Contents of a typical data package

Advantages of packet switching	Disadvantages of packet switching
• Packets do not need a dedicated line. • If a route is blocked or busy, the packet takes an alternative route. • Efficient as if any one packets fails to arrive, only that one packet needs to be resent. • Tends to be error free.	• Packets may arrive in the wrong order. • Can cause a delay until all packets have arrived. • Large memory needed to hold packets until all the message is assembled.

Check your understanding

REVISED

Without peeking, write the purpose of each of the devices in the table below.

Hardware	Purpose
Router	
Hub	
Switch	
Bridge	
Gateway	

Protocols

REVISED

A protocol is a set of rules. In communication between computers, the protocols must cover a number of factors otherwise the millions of different electronic devices all over the world would not understand each other.

There are many different protocols to cover every type of communication, such as Ethernet, email and internet communications.

In general, a communication protocol created for two devices to communicate should contain
- a handshake where one device asks if they can communicate and the other device says, 'go ahead'
- the type of error checking to be used
- data compression method, if used
- how the sending device will indicate that it has finished sending
- how the receiving device will indicate that it has received the message.

Different protocols are required for different reasons. The table below describes some of them.

Exam tip

Make sure you are familiar with all these protocols.

Protocol	Description
Ethernet	Describes how network devices can format data for transmission using frames and packets along a wired network and the standards for types of network cabling used.
Wifi	Describes how wireless signals can be sent and received. A common protocol is 801.11
TCP/IP	Transmission Control Protocol (TCP) and Internet Protocol (IP). These two distinct computer network protocols are used to send data packets around the internet.
HTTP	Hypertext Transfer Protocol describes the rules used to identify and transfer multimedia webpages over the internet.
HTTPS	Hypertext Transfer Protocol Secure is a secure form of HTTP; all data being transferred is encrypted.
FTP	File Transfer Protocol describes the rules used to transfer data from one computer to another through the internet.
SMTP	Simple Mail Transfer Protocol is for electronic mail (email) transmissions across the internet.
IMAP	Internet Message Access Protocol explains the rules for the transfers of emails between computer systems using the internet.

Layers

The TCP/IP protocols are a set of protocols know as **layers**. There are five layers to this model known as the TCP/IP 5-layer stack model. The layers are named
- physical layer
- data link layer
- network layer
- transport layer
- application layer.

Physical layer

- Transmits the raw data.
- Consists of hardware such as switches and routers.
- Deals with all aspects of setting up and maintaining a link between communicating computers.

Data Link Layer

- Sends data from the network layer to the physical layer.
- Divides the data to be sent into data frames.
- Handles the acknowledgements sent from the receiver.
- Ensures that incoming data has been received correctly.

Network layer

- Responsible for the addressing and routing of data.
- Includes routers as they use logical addresses to direct the data from the sender to the receiver.

Transport layer

- Ensures that data is transferred form one point to another reliably and without errors.
- Responsible for making sure that data is sent and received in the correct order.
- Acts as an interface between the communicating computers and the network.

Application layer

- Provides interfaces to the software to allow it to use the network.

Layers are used because

- if changes are made to one layer, the impact on the other layers is minimised
- protocol designers can work on a layer without worrying about how any new implementations may affect other layers
- it reduces a complex problem into several smaller parts making understanding the actions of each layer easier
- it makes troubleshooting easier to carry out as only the layer causing the problem needs working on
- it helps those developing products to make sure their product works with the other layers.

Routing

REVISED

Routing is the name given to the method of selecting paths along which packets are sent in a computer network. Routers, switches, bridges, firewalls and gateways construct a routing table, which stores several paths along which it is best to send the packets.

Devices will seek to choose the most economical route by looking for the
● shortest route to the destination
● fastest nodes.

Check your understanding

REVISED

1 Cover the right-hand side of the table on page 20 and check that you know the meaning of all the abbreviations on the left.
2 Jot down the names of the five layers in the TCP/IP system. Make sure you have them in the correct order.
3 Write down a definition of a protocol.
4 Write down a definition of a computer handshake.

IP addresses

REVISED

An IP address is an address using the Internet Protocol, which can uniquely identify every device on the internet, thus allowing communication between them. Every website has a unique IP address.

A device is allocated an IP address by a DHCP (Dynamic Host Configuration Protocol) server.

Internet Domain Name System (DNS)

A **Domain Name System** (DNS) is a database that matches IP addresses to computer system resources. IP addresses are not human friendly.

An example is 173.194.34.191.

The DNS server works as follows:
● The user types the website's name into a browser.
● The browser sends it to a DNS server.
● The server checks in its database and finds the corresponding IP address.
● This unique address is then used to route you to the appropriate webpage.

There are many different DNS servers located across the world. If your local DNS server does not store the address of the resource you are requesting, it will pass the request along to another higher-level DNS server, such as your internet server provider's (ISP) DNS server. If the address is not found again, your ISPs DNS server will pass the request on to a higher level DNS server which may be the DNS server responsible for an entire zone, such as the .co.uk zone. This continues until the address is found or the DNS query fails.

> **Exam tip**
>
> Remember that the world wide web is not the same as the internet. The www is a vast collection of websites; the internet is the network of networks that allow the www to exist.

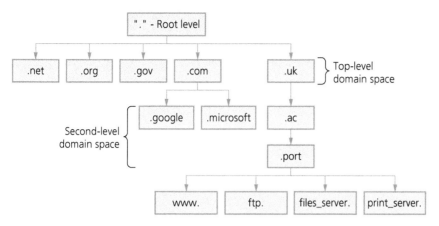

Figure 1.3.6 Domain space hierarchical structure

Now test yourself

TESTED

1 a) Sketch the following network topologies.
      i) Star   ii) Mesh   [2]
   b) Name two other network topologies.   [2]
2 a) Name the five layers in the TCP/IP protocol.   [5]
   b) Explain the importance of layers in TCP/IP.   [3]
3 Name **three** items contained in an IP Packet and describe how each one is used.   [3]

Answers available online

4 Organisation and structure of data

Data consists of any **character**, which is any letter, number, punctuation mark or symbol that can be typed on a computer keyboard. Data may also be in the form of pictures, video or sound.

The computer only works in 0s and 1s. A number system which only uses 0 or 1 is known as a binary system, sometimes called **base two**.

A computer must be told how to represent each character in **binary**.

Representation of numbers

Humans use a number system based on the number of fingers and thumbs on our hands. That is base ten. In fact, there are three main number systems that a computer scientist must know: binary, denary and hexidecimal.

Number system	Base	Example of base notation
Binary	Base 2	14_2
Denary	Base 10	14_{10}
Hexadecimal	Base 16	14_{16}

Denary	Binary	Hexadecimal
0	0000	0
1	0001	1
2	0010	2
3	0011	3
4	0100	4
5	0101	5
6	0110	6
7	0111	7
8	1000	8
9	1001	9
10	1010	A
11	1011	B
12	1100	C
13	1101	D
14	1110	E
15	1111	F
16	10000	10

We use
- binary numbers because that is what the computer understands
- denary numbers because that is what the human understands
- hexadecimal numbers as a shorthand for binary to make the long binary numbers easier to write, pronounce and work with (for example, it is easier to say FF than to say 11111111).

A computer scientist needs to know how to convert between the number bases.

For example, $1100_2 = C_{16} = 12_{10}$

To convert denary to binary

1 Divide the denary number successively by two until no more division is possible.
2 Read the remainders from the bottom to the top.

Example

Convert 35_{10} into binary.

$35 \div 2 = 17$, remainder is 1

$17 \div 2 = 8$, remainder is 1

$8 \div 2 = 4$, remainder is 0

$4 \div 2 = 2$, remainder is 0

$2 \div 2 = 1$, remainder is 0

$1 \div 2 = 0$, remainder is 1

Reading from the bottom up we get 100011

Therefore, $35_{10} = 100011_2$

To convert denary to hexadecimal

1 Divide the denary number successively by 16 until no more division is possible.
2 Read the remainders from the bottom to the top.

Example

Convert 49_{10} into hexadecimal.

$49 \div 16 = 3$, remainder is 1

$3 \div 16 = 0$, remainder is 3

Reading from the bottom up we get 31.

Therefore, $49_{10} = 31_{16}$

To convert binary to denary

1 Write down the binary number.
2 Multiply each digit of the binary number by the corresponding power of two.
3 Add the answers.

Example

Convert 100111_2 to denary.

$1 \times 32 + 0 \times 16 + 0 \times 8 + 1 \times 4 + 1 \times 2 + 1 \times 1$
$= 32 + 0 + 0 + 4 + 2 + 1$
$= 39_{10}$

> **Exam tip**
>
> You can use the table on the previous page to help you convert between binary and denary or to check your answers.

128	64	32	16	8	4	2	1

To convert binary to hexadecimal

1 Write down the binary number.
2 Group all the digits in sets of four, starting from the right.
3 Add zeros to the left of the last digit if there aren't enough digits to make a set of four.
4 Convert each group of four digits to denary.
5 Change the denary digits into hexadecimal (remember that the denary numbers 0–9 are the same as hexadecimal numbers, but that 10–15 translate to A–F).

Example

Convert 101110_2 to hexadecimal.

101110

$= 0010\ 1110$

$= 2_{10}\quad 14_{10}$

$= 2E_{16}$

Hexadecimal to denary

1 Write down the hexadecimal number.
2 Multiply each digit of the hexadecimal number by the corresponding power of 16.
3 Add the answers.

Example

Convert $A3_{16}$ to denary.

A3

$= A \times 16 + 3 \times 1$
$= 10 \times 16 + 3 \times 1$
$= 160 + 3$
$= 160 + 3$

$A3_{16} = 163_{10}$

Hexadecimal to binary

1 Write down the hexadecimal number with a good space between each digit.
2 Convert each number to a four-digit binary number, padding out with 0s if necessary. (You can use the table on page 24.)
3 Remove the space between the binary values and remove zeros at left (if necessary).

Example

Convert $2F_{16}$ to binary.

	2	F
$=$	0010	1111
$=$	00101111_2	
$=$	101111_2	

Check your understanding

Complete the table.

Denary	Binary	Hexadecimal
142		
	10011100	
		AE
161		
	101110101101	
		7A

Arithmetic shift functions

Computers cannot multiply in the same way that humans do. Instead they use **shift functions**.

The effect of a **left shift** is to double the number. Each time it is shifted left, it is doubled again.

Imagine that the table below represents an 8-bit register in a computer.

The computer is given the instruction to shift left.

Any digits leaving the register on the left disappear, gaps on the right are filled with 0s.

128	64	32	16	8	4	2	1	
0	0	0	1	1	1	0	1	Original number (29_{10})
0	0	1	1	1	0	1	0	First left shift (58_{10})
0	1	1	1	0	1	0	0	Second left shift (116_{10})

The process is
- one shift left multiplies by two
- two shifts left multiplies by four
- three shifts left multiplies by eight
- and so on.

A **right shift** instruction would have the effect of dividing by two.

In right shift operations, the gaps created on the left are filled with 0s and the bits on the right disappear as they leave the register.

Check your understanding

Complete the table to divide the binary number 00110100 by two and then by four.

Check that it works by calculating the denary equivalents.

128	64	32	16	8	4	2	1	
0	0	1	1	0	1	0	0	Original number (52_{10})
								First right shift ($\_\_\__{10}$)
								Second right shift ($\_\_\__{10}$)

Overflow

REVISED

Computers have fixed size registers. In shift operations and additions, bits disappear to the left or right. These bits are known as **overflow** bits.

Computers have special registers to note these overflows, to help keep calculations accurate. In these registers, certain bits known as **flags** will be set to remind the computer that a certain overflow has occurred.

Adding binary numbers

REVISED

Binary numbers are added in the same was as denary. However, with binary, as you go left, each bit is worth twice as much as the bit on the right; in denary, each number is worth 10 times the number on the right.

Example

$1101 + 1001$

	1	1	0	1	
	1	0	0	1	+
1	**0**	**1**	**1**	**0**	**Answer**
1			1		Carry bit

Notice that the left-hand bit would be an overflow if the computer only had a 4-bit register.

Check your understanding

REVISED

1 Calculate

0	0	0	1	1	1	1	1	
0	0	0	1	0	0	1	1	+
								Answer
								Carry bit

2 Calculate

1	0	0	0	1	1	0	1	
0	0	1	1	1	0	0	1	+
								Answer
								Carry bit

Representation of graphics and sound

REVISED

Digital storage of graphics

Graphics are stored as either bitmaps or vectors.

Bitmap graphics

- Graphics are made up of pixels (dots); each pixel has a position and a colour.
- The pixels are very small, but when so many are placed together they fool the human eye into thinking they are connected.
- The larger the graphic, the more pixels are needed to maintain the quality.
- Bitmap graphics are sometimes known as raster graphics.
- Bitmaps cannot be scaled up without a loss of quality. This is known as pixelation.
- Each individual pixel can be edited.

Vector graphics

- Vector graphics consist of equations that describe the relative distance of a point from the point of origin.
- Components are also described by length, thickness and colour.
- Vector graphics can be enlarged to any size without any loss in quality.
- Vector graphic file sizes are smaller than bitmaps and take up less storage space and are faster to load.

Digital storage and sampling of sound

- Sound can be stored in an analogue format (such as in vinyl records) or in a digital format (where the sound waves are **digitised**).
- The digitised files might be .wav or .mp3 files.
- These files can then be saved on CD, DVD, hard drives or flash memories.
- Digital representation of the sound is achieved by **sampling**.

Sampling

- Digital sound is recorded by taking a sample of the amplitude of the sound at a specific time; this amplitude is then recorded as a binary number.
- The greater the number of samples per second taken, the better the quality of the sound when played back.
- The greater the number of samples per second taken, the larger the file size.
- A common sample rate for music is 44 100 samples per second.

Figure 1.4.1 Original photograph of lamb, top, and pixellated image after enlargement, bottom.

Metadata

When graphic or sound files are stored, a lot of information about the file is stored too.

Some of this is of interest to the computer and computer programs, and some is of interest to the owner of the file.

Metadata for an image may include details of
- size of image
- dimensions of image
- camera used
- exposure time.

Figure 1.4.2 shows some of the many items recorded automatically when the image of the lamb (Figure 1.4.1) was taken and stored.

A sound file might record details such as name of song, name of artist and date of recording as metadata.

Figure 1.4.2 Metadata for lamb picture in Figure 1.4.1.

Check your understanding

Right click on any file and choose 'Properties' from the list available.

See what metadata is available for that file. It may surprise you how much there is.

Storage of characters

REVISED

All characters are stored in a computer or computer file as a binary number.

For instance

A could be 01100001

B could be 01100010

C could be 01100011

and so on.

Two common **character sets** are
- American Standard Code for Information Interchange (ASCII)
- Unicode.

By knowing the **standards** (such as Unicode or ASCII) used to record letters, a file can be sent to another computer where it would be understood. If we all made up our own codes to represent characters, we would never be able to read an email or transfer a file to another computer.

Each standard has its advantages and disadvantages. For instance, the ASCII set contains a limited number of characters but does not use many bits. Unicode has more characters but uses more memory.

Data types

REVISED

Data is stored in the computer in binary form as a series of 0s and 1s. In order to process the data, the computer needs to know the data type.

The common data types are shown below.

Data type	Example	Description
Number (integer)	43, –3	A whole number (positive or negative but no fractions)
Number (Real)	432.51, 11.2, –99.1	Any number including whole numbers and fractions
Boolean	Yes, True	The data can have only two possible outcomes such as 'Yes' or 'No', 'True' or 'False', 'Male' or 'Female'
Character	A, c, #, ?, 3	Any single character
String	John Smith, 2nh23bh2	

Data structures

REVISED

Data structures are used to hold data in a computer in a way that individual items within the structure can be easily accessed. The structures also preserve an order to the data.

These structures may be
- records
- arrays.

A **record** is a collection of related items, such as you might find in an address book.

A record consists of a number of **fields**. In an address book these fields might be

- first name
- last name
- address
- birthday.

The address book would be a collection of records, called a **file**, a **database**, or a **table**.

An **array** holds data in such a way that items can be found individually or accessed consecutively.

An array can be

- one-dimensional
- two-dimension
- n-dimensional.

Array A is a one-dimensional array.

	0	1	2	3	4	5	6	7	8
Array A	12	33	5	26	143	2	78	33	3

It contains nine elements contained in **cells** A(0) to A(8).

A(7) = 33

A(0) = 12

Array B is a two-dimensional array.

	0	1	2	3	4	5	6	7	8	
Array B	12	31	5	26	143	2	78	33	3	Row 0
	3	19	32	5	1	67	123	5	99	Row 1

With a two-dimensional array, there needs to be two references to identify an element.

You need to know the convention applying to the array – which is named first, the column or the row? In this case, it is row then column.

B(1,2) = 32

B(0,6) = 78

A one-dimensional array could be used for recording a series of temperatures of a liquid in an experiment.

A two-dimensional array could be used to record a series of temperatures and the densities of a liquid in an experiment.

Records and arrays can be manipulated or **edited**, where individual elements can be

- added
- deleted
- altered.

File design

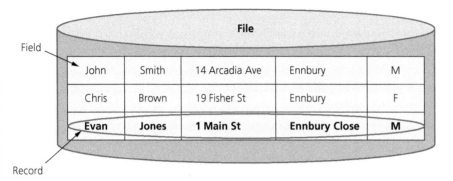

Field

	File			
John	Smith	14 Arcadia Ave	Ennbury	M
Chris	Brown	19 Fisher St	Ennbury	F
Evan	**Jones**	**1 Main St**	**Ennbury Close**	**M**

Record

Figure 1.4.4 How files, records and fields are related

- A **field** is a single data item.
- A **record** consists of a collection of related fields.
- A **file** is a collection of related records. In some databases they are referred to as **tables**.

Data validation and verification

Validation

Data entered into a computer record or array must be sensible, or we get inaccurate results or information when the data structure is interrogated. Validation rules are created to check that data being entered is sensible. As the data is entered, it is checked to see that it obeys the rules, and any data that does not will not be accepted. There are a number of such rules.

- A range check ensures that the data entered is within a sensible range.
- A type check ensures that the data is of the correct data type.
- A length check ensures that the number of characters entered does not exceed the allowed number.
- A lookup list or table checks the data entered against a limited number of possible entries.
- A format check ensures that the data being entered has a particular pattern, such as a postcode or a car registration number.
- A presence check ensures that certain data is present.
- A check digit is produced by applying an algorithm to the other digits in the number. The check digit is then appended to that number.

Verification

Verification is used to check that data copied into the computer is exactly the same as that on the source document.

There are two types of verification.
- **Visual verification**, where the source document is matched to the entered data by eye.
- **Double data entry**, where the data is typed by two different people and the two entries are compared by the computer to make sure that they match.

> **Exam tip**
>
> Validation is checking that data is sensible. Verification is checking that data has been copied correctly. It is not possible to check that the data is correct.

Proofreading

Proofreading is **not** a form of verification. It is used to check that a document contains grammatically correct, appropriate and correctly spelt material.

Algorithms

An algorithm is a series of steps designed to show how a process is carried out.

It can be in a diagrammatic form, or in the form of a computer program.

Imagine that a programmer wanted to validate an entry into a computer system. The numbers were only allowed to be between 1 and 100 inclusive. Any number outside this range would be rejected. The programmer first designs an algorithm in the form of a diagram.

Now test yourself

1   Complete the following data structure for a school record.   [10]

Field	Data type	Sample data	Validation check
First name	String	John	Presence check
Last name		Evans	
Form		3F	
House		Cardiff	
Gender		Male	
Number of siblings in school		2	

2   Describe the difference between a raster and vector graphics file.   [4]

Answers available online

5 System software

System software consists of programs designed to
- control the operations of the computer
- provide a platform for application software
- control peripheral devices.

The operating system

The operating system is a suite of system programs which manage the computer resources.

There are many different operating systems. Some of those commonly used are
- Windows
- MS-DOS
- Linux
- Apple macOS.

An operating system will manage
- peripherals, such as keyboards, mice, printers, monitors and other input or output devices attached to the computer
- printing and scanning, using spooling
- storage devices, such as disc drives, DVDs and flash memory
- immediate access stores, such as RAM and ROM
- utility programs, such as disk defragmenters
- all the processes currently taking place in the computer
- security of the computer against virus attacks for instance.

The operating system provides a **user interface**. This is where the human and the computer interact. This is known as the **human computer interface** (HCI). An HCI
- allows copying, deleting, moving, sorting and searching of files or folders
- allows access to system settings, such as hardware
- provides a command line interface
- allows users to have more than one window open
- provides a graphical user interface (windows, icons, menus, pointers)
- identifies errors and help messages
- allows customisation of the interface, such as changes to desktop background and layout
- allows user to switch between tasks.

The interface could be
- a **graphical user interface** (GUI)
- a **command line interface** (CLI).

Graphical user interface

A GUI is an intuitive interface. It is a user-friendly system, meaning that most people are able to operate the system without too much training.

Most modern computers operate in this way, using a **WIMP** environment.
- A **window** is a rectangular area of the screen in which an application runs.
- An **icon** is a small picture on the screen to help identify the program or shortcut.

- A **menu** is a list of options.
- A **pointer** is an image moved across the screen by a mouse (often a little arrow head).

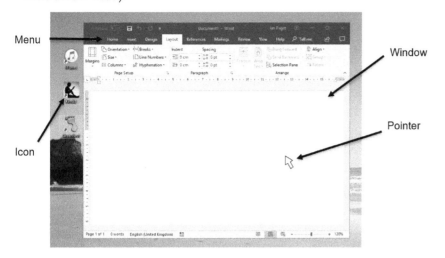

Menu

Window

Icon

Pointer

Figure 1.5.1 A WIMP interface

Command line interface

A command line interface is designed to allow a user to type in commands at a prompt. The operating system will then execute that command.

Users can use simple commands at the prompt to carry out functions such as
- copy files
- delete files
- move files to different folders
- sort files into order
- search for a particular file or folder.

With a CLI, there is more control than there is with a GUI, as the user is directly accessing the operating system. This allows the user to access system settings and hardware directly.

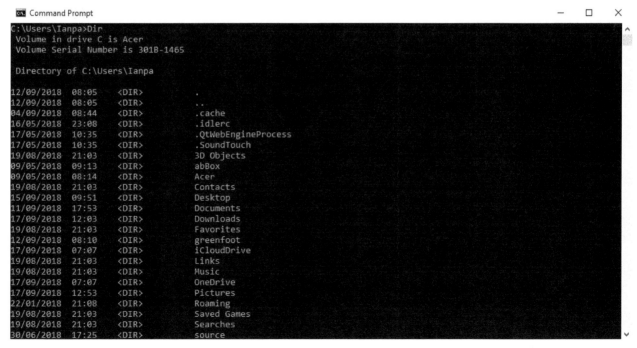

Figure 1.5.2 A CLI interface

The operating system on most computers will
- allow the user to have more than one window open at the same time, including having a CLI and a GUI window open
- provide useful error messages
- provide help
- allow a user to customise the GUI interface, change desktop background and layout
- allow a user to switch between tasks; for example, have a spreadsheet and a word processor open at the same time.

Check your understanding

1 Check that you understand the difference between CLI and GUI interfaces.
2 Find out how to open the CLI on your computer and type DIR followed by return to see what files are listed.
3 In your GUI move the cursor around on the screen and look at the different shapes the pointer takes depending on what applications are open.

Utility software

Certain useful system programs are called **utility software**. These programs are able to do 'housekeeping' jobs to keep the computer running efficiently. Some utility programs are shown below.
- **Virus scanners** help to keep the computer safe from attacks by a computer virus by
  - continually scanning the computer files looking for anomalies
  - quarantining a potential virus found in a file
  - informing the user and asking if they wish the file to be deleted
  - continually updating itself to remain useful.
- A **firewall** is software that can help prevent hackers from accessing the system by
  - monitoring all the data traffic coming in and out of the computer
  - blocking all data from unknown sources
  - allowing limited public access to the computer
  - allowing the user to define the rules for which sites are allowed access and which are banned.
- **Defragmentation** software rearranges the data on a disc to make it more efficient by
  - identifying where gaps begin to appear as files are added and deleted on a disc
  - moving the parts of files around so as to make the sections of a file **contiguous** as sometimes there is no space big enough on the disc to hold it
  - helping files to be loaded more quickly as the read head does not have to jump around looking for different parts of the file.
- **Compression** software
  - reduces the sizes of files for storage or transmission
  - decompresses compressed files to restore them to ordinary use.
- **System monitoring** software allows certain performance details of the computers performance to be displayed such as
  - observing and tracking the activities of users
  - reporting on the applications running on the system
  - showing the processes that are being performed on a computing system.

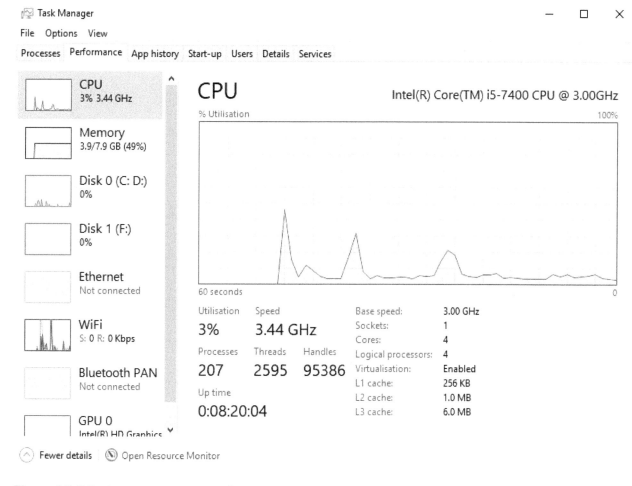

Figure 1.5.3 System management software

- **Task management** software monitors the performance and the resources being used by the currently running tasks.
- **Disk scanning and repair** software can find faulty parts of a disc and try to repair it by
  - checking the hard drive for sector errors
  - attempting to fix the error
  - moving the data to another location on the disk which is not damaged
  - removing a sector that cannot be repaired from the memory map so that it is not used again.
- **Backup** software makes regular copies of the data stored on a disc by allowing the user to
  - decide which files to backup
  - decide where to store the backup copy, such as offsite in a secure location
  - schedule the frequency of the backups.

Check your understanding

REVISED

Press CTR–ALT–DEL and click on task manager to see how your system is being monitored.

Now test yourself

1 Describe **four** features of the operating system when providing a GUI on a personal computer. Give a
   suitable example of each feature.   [8]
2 Tick True or False to indicate if the task is carried out by the operating system.   [8]

Task	True	False
Spellchecking		
Managing the printer		
Dealing with errors		
Sorting records		
Setting tabs		
Handling the storage of data		
Managing emails		
Organising resources		

3 Describe the function and purpose of each of the following system maintenance tools in
   a computer system   [4]
   ● Disk Compression
   ● Defragmentation
4 Describe the role of the operating system when managing system resources.   [4]
5 Identify and describe **four** roles of the operating system when managing the resources of
   a personal computer.   [8]

Answers available online

6 Principles of programming

Computer languages

Computer languages are classified as being
- low-level
- high-level.

High-level languages

High-level languages use programming statements that generally resemble English or mathematical expressions. This is sometimes called program code.

Programmers prefer to use high-level languages as they
- are generally easier to use and understand than low-level languages
- are problem-orientated which facilitates creating programs for a particular use or problem
- have built-in functions
- have single commands that can carry out complex tasks
- are similar to natural spoken language
- can use meaningful and complex variable names
- can be run on different computer platforms.

Many high-level languages are written with a 'write once run anywhere' (WORA) philosophy.

Examples of high-level languages are
- **Java**, a general purpose, object-oriented language
- **Python**, used specifically for code readability and very useful when coding in teams or working collaboratively
- **Visual Basic**, used for writing programs with a graphical user interface
- **Cobol**, used in the finance and business world
- **Lisp**, used to program mathematical logic.

High-level languages have facilities that are not found in low-level languages, these include
- selection structures, such as IF, THEN, ELSE and CASE statements
- iteration structures, such as WHILE, REPEAT, UNTIL, FOR
- built-in routines, such as functions
- data types, such as real, integer, float, Boolean and char
- data structures, such as array and stack.

Examples of functions in Java for instance are
- MsgBox()
- readLine() and writeLine()
- mathematical functions such as sqr(), log(), chr().

An example segment of a high-level program written in Java:

```
public class IfExample {
public static void main(String[] args) {
    int age=16;
    if(age→16){
    System.out.print("You are old enough to drive a
car");
    }
}
}
```

Low-level languages

Low-level languages are machine orientated. So, when programming, the programmer has to have in mind the architecture of the processor rather than the problem to be solved.

They are generally used by specialist programmers when the priority is to produce code that
- executes as fast as possible
- occupies as little memory as possible.

The lowest level language is **machine code** which is written entirely in binary using multiple copies of 0 and 1. Computers can only execute programs in binary machine code. In the beginning, programmers had to write programs in machine code.

A machine code program would look like this:

```
00101000
10110011
10010101
01001011
...
```

While it is possible to write programs directly in machine code, it is only generally used when there is a requirement to manipulate individual bits and bytes directly. Programming in machine code is difficult and tracking down errors (**debugging**) is very time consuming.

Machine code is used for creating
- device drivers for managing peripherals, such as scanners, printers and so on
- embedded systems, such as those used in
  - helping to control jet aircraft
  - monitoring motorcar performance
  - washing machines
  - televisions
  - burglar alarms.

Assembly language

Assembly language uses mnemonics (meaningful abbreviations) for the machine code instructions. Assembly languages are
- computer-orientated
- difficult for programmers to develop code and to test and code
- difficult to use as simple tasks need a lot of instructions

- used to develop programs that
  - ○ need to run very fast
  - ○ take up a minimum amount of space
  - ○ can be hard coded onto chips
  - ○ can be in full control of the CPU.

Each line of assembly language consists of an instruction (**opcode**) that may by followed by an item of data (**operand**). This is then executed during the fetch-decode-execute cycle.

Assembly language programs are more readable than binary code programs.

```
MOV AL,5
CLC
MOV AH,2
INT 21H
...
```

Check your understanding

Fill in the table by assigning the letters representing the statements to the correct column.

A   Machine code

B   Java

C   Assembly language

D   Important when speed is important, and memory is limited

E   Is closer to human spoken language

F   Contains built-in functions

High-level	Low-level

Now test yourself

1 a) Explain the difference between machine and assembly programming languages. [3]
   b) Name one high-level language and explain why programmers prefer high-level languages over low-level. [5]

Answers available online

7 Software engineering

Software engineering is a term which describes the process of developing software. This includes
- testing the software to make sure it works
- debugging, which is finding and correcting errors
- documentation so that other programmers can understand the code
- maintenance over time to keep the software up-to-date.

Software packages have been developed to help in the process of software engineering. This software is known as an **integrated development environment** (IDE) and provides programmers with tools to aid the development of a software program. An IDE can often support several programming languages.

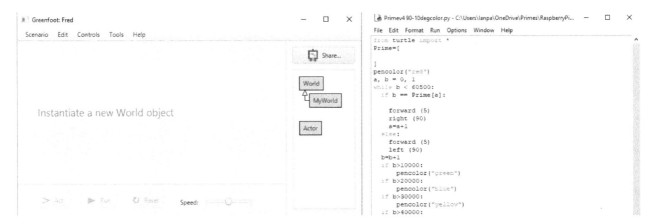

Figure 1.7.1 Greenfoot IDE (left) and Python IDE (right)

Here are some of the tools available within an IDE:
- An **editor** allows the programmer to enter and edit the high-level language source code. Used for the development of software, writing the code and designing the interface that will become the software program or application.
- A **compiler** converts the source code into executable object code (machine code). Once compiled, a program can be run at any time without needing to be recompiled.
- An **interpreter** converts each line of the source code into object code and executes it as it goes. The conversion process is performed each time the program needs to be run, meaning that the interpreter always needs to be present.
- A **linker** allows previously compiled (or assembled) sections of code to be linked together.
- A **loader** loads previously compiled (or assembled) object code into memory.

The IDE also contains **debugging tools**. Debugging is the process of identifying errors within the code to ensure it is executable.

The **debugger** is a program that helps to track down and identify any errors in a program.

Here are some of the tools within the debugger:

- **Trace** prints out or displays the order in which the lines of a program are executed, and possibly the values of variables as the program is being run.
- **Break point** interrupts a program at a specific line allowing the programmer to check the current value of a variable against the expected value.
- **Variable watch** also displays the current value of any variable. The value can be 'watched' as the program code is single-stepped to see the effects of the code on the variable.
- **Single-stepping** allows the program code to be executed one line at a time with the programmer deciding when the next step will take place, so as to examine carefully what the program is doing at that moment.
- **Store dump** displays the contents of all the stores used in the program.
- **Memory inspector** displays the contents of all the stores in a defined section of memory.
- **Error diagnostics** displays error messages to help the programmer diagnose what has gone wrong when a program fails to compile or to run successfully.

Now test yourself

TESTED

1 a) Identify and explain **three** tools a debugger uses to track down and identify errors within a program. [3]
   b) Name an IDE you have used.
      Identify and explain **three** tools available within the IDE. [4]

Answers available online

8 Program construction

Computers can only understand and execute machine code instructions; therefore, the code of all programming languages must be converted into machine code before the program can be run.

There are three programs that will do this conversion. They are known as translators because they will translate from, say, assembly code to machine code. The three programs are:
- assemblers
- compilers
- interpreters.

Assembler

- An assembler is a program that converts low-level language programs into executable code.
- Each mnemonic written by the programmer is replaced by the corresponding binary machine code instruction by the assembler.

Mnemonics

Machine code or binary code is hard to use. So, the assembly language uses symbols instead of thousands of 0s and 1s for each instruction. Some examples of instructions and their mnemonics are

Instruction	Mnemonic
INPUT	INP
OUTPUT	OUT
STORE	STA
LOAD	LDA
ADD	ADD
SUBTRACT	SUB
BRANCH	BRA
STOP	HLT

> **Exam tip**
>
> A mnemonic means using a pattern, symbol or code to aid remembering, such as LDA for load the accumulator.

Addressing

Every location in a computer memory has an address. If data is placed in any of the addresses, we have to remember which location contains which data.

Using an assembler, a name can be given to a location which makes the program more readable and helps the programmer remember where items of data are stored.

For example, instead of using location 108 to store the price of a bicycle, we could call the location bikeprice or bp.

Compiler

A **compiler** translates a complete program written in a high-level language known as the source code, such as C++, into machine code in one go without stopping.

- Each high-level instruction can generate many low-level ones.
- A compiler produces a program that can be run independently from the compiler.
- A list of errors is produced at the end of the process.

Advantages of a compiler

- A compiled program runs faster than an interpreted program.
- It checks all lines of coding whereas an interpreter only checks the ones executed.

Interpreter

REVISED

An **interpreter** analyses the source code line by line and converts it into machine code to be executed by the CPU.

- Each high-level instruction may generate several low-level instructions.
- The program can only run if the interpreter is present.
- If an error is encountered, the interpreter stops and shows the error.

Advantages of an interpreter

- Allows easier program development as errors can be corrected as the program is being interpreted.
- Individual lines of code can be modified at run time.

The process of compilation

REVISED

The compilation can be split into **five** stages:
1 Lexical analysis
2 Syntax analysis
3 Semantic analysis
4 Code generation
5 Optimisation

Lexical analysis

- All comments and spaces are removed.
- All keywords, constants and identifiers used in the source code are replaced by 'tokens'.
- A symbol table is created which holds the addresses of variables, labels and subroutines.

Syntax analysis

- Each statement is checked against the rules of syntax for the assembler.
  - Each statement is checked for spelling.
  - Each statement is checked for grammar.
  - Each statement is checked to see that the sequence of input characters, symbols, items or tokens obey the rules of syntax of the language.
- Parsing is the task of systematically breaking down, during the translation process, the high-level language statements into their component parts, such as reserved words and variables.

Semantic analysis

- Checking that the meanings of the statements are clear and consistent with the rules of the compiler, the structure and data types that are supposed to be used.
- Making checks to see if all variables used in the program have been declared.
- Carrying out type checks to see, for instance, that real values have not been assigned to integer variables.
- Checking that appropriate operations have been carried out on variables; for example, that integer division has not been carried out on real variables.

Code generation

- Generating the machine code. Most high-level language statements will be translated into several machine code instructions.

Optimisation

- Employing a technique to attempt to reduce the execution time of the object program.

Programming errors

REVISED

When a program is written, there are nearly always errors, however careful the programmer has been.

Syntax errors

- Occur when the program is being compiled and the code does not follow the expected syntax of the language; in many cases this is caused by a spelling mistake or by not closing brackets.
  For example, (A+6/3 is incorrect.
  The correct version should be (A+6)/3.

Linking errors

- May occur if a compiled program is linked to library routines. For example, a subroutine may not be present in the library.

Run-time errors

- Occur when the program is being run.
- Parts of the program work, but elements have been programmed incorrectly.
- When executed, this mistake causes the program to crash, known as a **run-time error**. For example, a program tries to display a user's name, but the name has not been saved anywhere and so causes the program to crash.

Now test yourself

TESTED

1 a) Describe **two** types of programming errors, giving specific examples of how these errors may occur. [4]

   b) Describe the **five** stages of the compilation process. [5]

   c) Explain what is meant by the term *Compiler*, noting its advantages and disadvantages. [5]

Answers available online

9 Security and data management

Data security

REVISED

Whenever personal data is stored electronically there are problems of security. Data held on personal computers can be in danger from several sources. These dangers include:

- hacking, where data may be deliberately changed, stolen or deleted by unauthorised people
- a computer virus affecting the data
- the hard drive may crash, or some other vital component fail
- interception of data when being transferred from device to device such as by email
- stealing data from old hard drives, CDs, and so on that have been thrown away (in one case, a man threw away a hard drive containing a bitcoin wallet worth millions of pounds).

To keep the data safe, precautions must be taken, such as:

- setting **access rights** to files where files can be set so that users other than yourself have
  - no access
  - read access
  - read and write access
- choosing suitable **passwords** that are
  - strong – containing a mixture of upper and lowercase letters, digits and special symbols
  - changed regularly
  - not related to any personal details like dates of birth or pet names
  - never revealed to anyone
- **encryption** that scrambles data to prevent it being understood if it is intercepted; the data is changed so that a hacker will not be able to understand it.

Data management

REVISED

Data needs to be carefully managed. This means that you will need to
- use sensibly named folders and files
- store files and folders in a logical way so that you can find them again
- take precautions against the loss of any data files by
  - accident
  - hacking.

Precautions against permanently losing data can be taken by making **backups** and **archiving** files that are no longer used.

Backing up data involves making a copy of the data on a regular basis and storing the backup copy off-site or on a detachable medium such as flash disc, tape or DVD in a secure location.

Some larger institutions use a backup procedure known as the **grandfather, father, son method** sometimes called creating **generations** of files.

> **Exam tip**
>
> Archived data is data no longer in current use but is saved for legal, security or historical reasons.

The most recent copy of the data is the **son** file. If an error occurs in processing the son file, the **father** file can be used. The oldest version of the files is the **grandfather** file, which is called on if both the father and the son have failed.

Compression

Data compression frees up disc space by making files smaller. Image and sound files can be compressed by using **compression algorithms** known as **lossy** and **lossless** compression.

● Lossy compression results in reduction of data quality.
● Lossless compression results in no loss of data quality.

We can use data compression to help overcome problems with saving large files. Files can be compressed to make them smaller when stored or sent over a network, but they will need to be decompressed before they can be used.

Data compression	
Advantages	**Disadvantages**
● smaller file size, so files will take up less storage space when saved on hard disk or other storage media	● precision can be lost
● files will reach their destination more quickly when sent over a network or up/downloaded over the internet	● it is not always possible to return to the uncompressed state

The ratio by which compression reduces a file size is known as the **compression ratio**.

$$\text{The compression ratio} = \frac{\text{original file size}}{\text{compressed file size}}$$

Example

An image is reduced from 800 MB to 80 MB. Work out the compression ratio.

$$\text{The compression ratio} = \frac{\text{original file size}}{\text{compressed file size}} = \frac{800}{80} = \frac{10}{1} \text{ or } 10:1$$

Figure 1.9.1 Uncompressed image (left), with increasing compression to the right

The parrot image on the left had an original image size of 2 MB.

The middle parrot image was compressed to 270 KB.

The parrot on the right was further compressed to 176 KB.

No apparent changes to the image can be seen by the human eye.

However, if the images were enlarged, the right hand image would become pixellated sooner than the others.

Check your understanding

1 Give **three** characteristics of a strong password.
2 A file has been treated using a compression algorithm using a compression ratio of 7 : 1. The compressed file has a size of 50 KB. Calculate the original file size.

Network security

Networks are used by a lot of people and are often connected to the internet. This means that the data stored there can be at risk of
● hacking
● virus installation
● malware
● spyware
● trojans
● worms
● technical breakdown
● interception of data as it is moved from place to place.

It is, therefore, vital to keep the network and data as secure as possible.

Security tools have been developed to help keep the network secure. These include
● installation and use of regularly updated **anti-virus** software
● **firewalls** that monitor all the data going in and out of a computer and can help prevent hackers from accessing the system
● **two-factor authentication** that adds an item of personal information – in addition to a password – that only the legitimate user would know, such as a code texted to a phone
● **access levels** to different areas of the network or hard drive; for example, a teacher could access all of the students' work, but the student could only access their own.
● **passwords** to restrict access to programs, data and different access levels.

Policies

There needs to be a policy in place so that everyone knows how to cope in the event of a disaster where all work is potentially lost, such as a fire in the building. This is the **disaster recovery policy**.

A disaster recovery policy attempts to find ways to
● minimise interruptions to normal operations
● limit the extent of disruption and damage
● establish alternative means of working so staff know exactly how to proceed
● provide for smooth and rapid restoration of service.

There should also be an **acceptable use policy**, which is a set of rules applied by the manager of the data or administrator of a network. This sets out the guidelines of how the system should be used. This is usually a list of unacceptable uses such as

- visiting obscene websites
- downloading or uploading obscene images
- handling material that some may find offensive
- sending unsolicited emails (spam).

Cybersecurity

Cybersecurity is the

- state of being protected against the criminal use of electronic data
- measures taken to achieve this protection.

Nationally cybersecurity is taken very seriously. In Britain, the **National Cyber Security Centre (NCSC)** is part of the GCHQ complex in Cheltenham.

The NCSC was set up to

- help protect the Nation's critical services from cyber attacks
- manage major incidents
- improve the underlying security of the UK's internet
- give advice to citizens and organisations
- help make the UK the safest place to live and do business online.

Network administrators must be prepared to fight off attacks from a number of sources.

These include

- malicious software (**malware**); malware is a term used to describe any software that could be used to disrupt a computer operation or compromise a user
- **viruses**, which are computer programs that can copy themselves onto other programs; they often attempt to damage the existing data, fill the hard drive or cause a computer to shut down unexpectedly
- **worms**, which are like viruses but replicate themselves in order to spread to other computers; they can copy themselves and 'worm' their way through a system
- **key loggers**, which capture the keystrokes a user makes on the keyboard and sends this data to a third party for misuse.

In addition to systems such as firewalls and anti-virus programs, protection can be had from

- keeping software updated regularly
- using security tools such as password strength checkers or advertisement blockers
- training personnel to take sensible precautions such as not inserting a flash memory handed to them by a stranger.

Technical weaknesses

Even if a system has all the cybersecurity mentioned, there are still technical weaknesses that can be exploited by someone with intent of doing harm, such as a hacker.

Technical weakness	
SQL injection	A hacker places some malicious code into a SQL statement in your database.
DoS attack	A **denial of service** attack where your computer system becomes unavailable to the intended users. Sometimes caused by bombarding the system with emails.
Password attack	These could be a **brute force attack** where the hacking algorithm tries all kinds of combinations until it finds one that fits, or a **dictionary attack** where the hacking software systematically tries every word in a dictionary until it finds an accepted password.
IP address spoofing	A false IP address is put into a data packet to hide the real identity of the sender.
Social engineering	Online manipulation of someone to encourage them to divulge confidential information.
Phishing	Attempting to gain confidential or personal information by pretending to be an official site, such as a bank.
Footprinting	Hackers try to find out everything they can about a system.

Protecting software during production

REVISED

While software is being developed it goes through the stages of
- design
- creation
- testing
- use.

During any of these stages, the software can be vulnerable. Methods of combatting these vulnerabilities include
- not allowing buffer overflow when creating an input
- checking string formats on input looking for disallowed characters
- making sure that all parameters used in functions are validated.

Internet cookies

REVISED

A **cookie** is a small amount of data generated by a website and saved by your web browser. It can remember information about you, what you entered on the site and how you used it. The idea is that this information can then be used to prepare customised web pages or to save login information so that you automatically log in when you load the page.

Because cookies hold personal information they could be a security issue.

It is probably a good idea to clear cookies from your computer from time to time.

Now test yourself

TESTED

1 a) Describe how a lossy algorithm could be implemented to compress a sound file. [2]
   b) A sound file is 640 KB. Following compression its file size is reduced to 64 KB. Calculate the compression ratio. [2]
2 a) Describe **two** types of potential cyber security threats and methods of protection against these threats. [3]
   b) Describe the dangers that can arise using computer networks within a school and discuss measures/steps the network administrator can take to ensure suitable security of the network. [6]

Answers available online

10 Ethical, legal and environmental impacts

Digital technology has a wide impact on society. The digital revolution has touched everywhere in the world. Almost no one is immune to the effects of the digital revolution that has taken place in the last 30 years or so.

Computer crime

Several crimes are associated with the widespread use of computers.

Identity theft

Identity theft can occur through **phishing**. Phishing is when an email is sent to you that appears to come from an official organisation, such as a bank, asking you to send personal details, such as passwords and your bank account number. The purpose is to steal your identity and empty your bank account.

To prevent identity theft
- never give out bank details or passwords on emails
- do not throw away receipts, bills or statements without tearing them up or shredding them first
- check your bank and credit card statements regularly
- make sure nobody watches you when you enter a PIN at an ATM
- do not write down passwords
- change passwords regularly.

Computer viruses

These can attack computer data, attempt to steal passwords, cause annoying adverts to appear or track online movements.

Guard against computer viruses by
- only using reputable websites
- installing and using virus protection software (anti-virus)
- never downloading illegal copies of software
- updating your anti-virus software regularly.

The business of keeping us and our data safe online is known as cybersecurity.

> **Exam tip**
>
> A cryptographer helps to encrypt data so that it is meaningless unless you have a key to decode it.

E-commerce

Businesses are able to offer their goods and services to people in any part of the world through websites. These websites can be viewed by anybody in any country, provided they have a device with internet access. People can also buy goods from companies overseas by ordering through a website.

This globalisation of business has advantages and disadvantages.

Advantages

● Expanded markets.
● Allowing companies to streamline their operations so they can employ fewer people.
● Decreasing companies' expenses.
● Goods can be shipped directly from a warehouse to the customer's doorstep.
● Maximised profits.

Disadvantages

● People lose jobs.
● Shops on the high street disappear.
● Managers that used to run shops now work online.
● Reduced utility bills and property taxes paid to councils.

It can be argued that rich countries are gaining at the expense of poorer countries whose shares of the global market are extremely small. This is known as the digital divide. However, mobile telephones and wider use of computers is helping poorer communities and, in some countries, driving revolution for change.

Social impact of digital technology

REVISED

More people are working from home, saving on expenditure of fuel and time, but the home still has to be heated and digital equipment used. There is a balance between the energy saved by not heating and lighting offices and saving on travelling, and having every worker heating and lighting their homes all day and having more time for leisure, travel and shopping.

Digital devices are making it easier to monitor what people are doing.
● CCTV cameras are everywhere in towns and cities.
● Communications from phone calls, emails and text messages can be monitored.
● Satellites with cameras are capable of seeing what you are reading or identify a car number plate.
● Google® Earth lets anyone see anywhere on Earth or virtually travel the streets of unfamiliar towns.
● Mobile phone signals and debit and credit card use can be used to track our movements.
● We voluntarily leave our thoughts and pictures on Facebook, YouTube, Twitter and other social media.
● Most governments are creating databases of DNA.
● Many governments have introduced identity cards and biometric passports.

We should ask:
● do these issues effect our human rights?
● do we have a right to privacy?
● can we question to what extent should our privacy be affected?
● is it OK to breach our rights to privacy to protect others (for example, to prevent terrorist attacks)?

It is important that laws are passed to protect the individual from these threats to their privacy and there needs to be a balance between what is beneficial (such as cutting down crime) and what is harmful (invasion of privacy).

The use of computer data helps to form political opinion with survey groups, such as YouGov, allowing politicians and businesses to constantly monitor how people are thinking and to change the way they govern accordingly.

The internet allows the public to share experiences all over the world. This has meant that different groups can air their views to the world, and radio and television broadcasts – especially news – can be seen and heard anywhere in the world.

In 2011, it became possible to fill in the census online and, in the future, it may be possible to vote in the UK from home using the internet.

Check your understanding

REVISED

1 Describe some of the jobs created by using ICT in the workplace.
2 List the social changes brought about by ICT in our everyday lives.

Standards

REVISED

It is important that society develops acceptable standards of behaviour online and when using digital equipment. Peer pressure will eventually drive how society thinks of behaviour online. We are all aware of the importance of staying safe online, but there is a certain ambivalence at the moment to
- online trolling
- sexting
- cyber-bullying
- stalking
- false news.

It is too easy to hide behind a false identity online and be able to get away with things that are ethically and morally unacceptable in ordinary life.

Many companies have formal codes of behaviour that workers must sign when they start their employment.

Schools try to educate scholars to do the ethical and moral things online.

Legislation

REVISED

Governments produce legislation which helps to prevent online crimes by making certain things illegal; breaking these rules incurs fines or imprisonment.

These laws could impact on our security, privacy, data protection and freedom of information and will help regulate how organisations treat our data.

Current United Kingdom legislation

General Data Protection Regulation (GDPR)

This EU law is part of the British Data Protection Act (2018). The GDPR deals with data held about an individual.

This is known as personal data. It is defined as any data that could identify an individual in any way. There are many organisations and businesses that hold our personal data, such as

- the HM Revenue and Customs (the tax office)
- a doctor or a dentist
- the Driver and Vehicle Licensing Agency (DVLA)
- any online shopping, gaming or social media site to which you sign up
- the police.

The GDPR refers to the **data subject**, the **data controller** and the **data processor**.

- The data subject is the individual whose personal data is stored on a computer.
- The data controller is the person in an organisation who decides the purpose of collecting the data and how it will be used.
- The data processor is the person in an organisation who processes the data on behalf of the data controller.

In smaller organisations, the data controller and the data processor may be the same person.

The GDPR defines some data as 'sensitive personal data' that must not be disclosed or processed without the data subject's knowledge and consent. Sensitive personal data includes data about the subject's

- racial or ethnic origin
- religious or philosophical beliefs
- political opinions
- trade union membership
- health
- genetic or biometric data
- sex life or sexual orientation.

There are some exceptions to the regulation. These include collection of data for

- national security
- detection of crime
- scientific or historical research
- processing wages, pensions or tax
- data used privately at home for household or recreational reasons.

Computer Misuse Act (1990)

The Computer Misuse Act (1990) is a law that makes it illegal to

- gain unauthorised access to files stored on a computer system, including viewing and copying the files
- gain unauthorised access to files and use them for criminal activities such as fraud or blackmail
- change or delete any files unless authorised to do so – this includes creating or planting viruses.

Electronic Communications Act (2000)

The Electronic Communications Act was passed to

- set up a register of cryptographers
- help e-commerce
- recognise digital signatures as legal.

Regulation of Investigatory Powers Act (2000)

The purpose of the Regulation of Investigatory Powers Act is to
- make it illegal to intercept emails, phone calls, letters and other communications without permission
- protect the individual from the state and means that groups, such as the police, cannot eavesdrop on conversations without special permission.

Freedom of Information Act (2000)

The Freedom of Information Act provides public access to information held by public authorities such as government departments, local authorities and the NHS by
- making authorities publish certain information about their activities, including printed documents, computer files, letters, emails, photographs and sound or video recordings
- allowing members of the public to request information from public authorities.

Copyright Designs and Patent Act (1988)

The Copyright (Computer Programs) Regulations 1992 extended the rules covering literary works to include computer programs. The Copyright Designs and Patent Act gives the creators the right to
- control the ways in which their material may be used
- be identified as the author
- object to distortions of the work
- withhold permission to the copying of the work
- demand a payment for the copying of the work.

Check your understanding

REVISED

1 Name **four** groups or organisations that are exempt from the GDPR.
2 Explain why it is necessary to have a Freedom of Information Act.
3 Describe what is meant by Sensitive Personal Data.

Environmental issues

REVISED

The environmental impact of computer use is greater than we think. We must be careful about the use of computing devices and the effect of this use on the environment.

Manufacture of computer equipment involves
- more energy used in homes
- factories worldwide using energy and resources to produce electronic items that are soon out of date and ready to be discarded
- using rare elements in the manufacture of most electronic devices; this means increased mining activities and disturbance of the natural environment
- huge amounts of energy to maintain online servers, cloud storage and keep the millions of networks forming the internet running.

The following can reduce the environmental impact of computer use:

- Use recycled paper or store documents on a hard drive rather than using paper to save the forest resources.
- Manage the life cycle of computer equipment carefully by upgrading where possible rather than replacing the entire piece. Manufacturing of computer equipment uses natural resources and generates carbon emissions.
- Dispose of old equipment carefully. Hardware contains a number of harmful elements. If the equipment is dumped in landfill, harmful chemicals can get into the water supply or contaminate living things.
- Reduce the amount of energy consumed by switching off the computer or peripheral devices when not in use. Set up energy saving schemes on the computer.
- Computer equipment tends to generate heat, so consider opening a window rather than switching on air-conditioning.
- Businesses should consider using video conferencing rather than sending delegates to meetings. This reduces the carbon footprint of these meetings by cutting down on travelling.

Now test yourself

TESTED ☐

1 a) Describe **two** types of crime the Computer Misuse Act is designed to prevent. [2]
  b) From the GDPR, name **three** items of personal data an organisation cannot disclose without permission, and **three** instances when exceptions can be made? [6]

Answers available online

Worked examples

Using the keyword give.

Question

Give **one** advantage and **one** disadvantage of circuit switching.　　　[2]

Answer

An advantage of circuit switching is that there is no delay in transmitting data once the circuit is complete.

A disadvantage is that the circuit cannot be used to transmit data to a different destination.

Commentary

*The keyword is **give**, so there is no need for any explanation.*

Only one mark is available for the advantage and one for the disadvantage, so don't write too much.

Make sure you indicate which of your answers refers to the disadvantage and which to the advantage.

Using the keyword state

Question

State the purpose of the accumulator in the CPU.　　　[1]

Answer

The accumulator is a register for short term storage.

Commentary

*The keyword is **state** and so no explanation is needed. Only one mark is available.*

Using the keyword identify

Question

Identify **two** components of a CPU.　　　[2]

Answer

Control unit

Arithmetic and logic unit

Commentary

*The keyword is **identify**, so you only need to name the components. There is no need to write a description.*

Using the keyword describe

Question

Describe the characteristics of a laser printer.   [3]

Answer

It is quieter to run than an impact printer.

It uses toner cartridges to produce the print.

It can produce a high number of pages per minute.

Commentary

*The keyword is **describe**, so answer in sentences. Three marks are given, so make sure that you give three distinct characteristics.*

Using the keyword explain

Question

Explain the concept of overflow when adding two binary numbers.   [4]

Answer

Computer registers have a fixed number of bits.

If a computer register has only 4 bits to represent a number, then the answer can only be shown using 4 bits.

For example, adding 1001 to 1101 gives 10110.

The answer is 5 bits long and so the most significant bit is lost to overflow.

An overflow register will note that an overflow has occurred.

Commentary

*The keyword is **explain**, so there are several marks available. It is often useful to give an example to help with your explanation.*

There are four marks so you must make at least four points to gain the marks.

Using the keyword compare

Question

Compare RAM and ROM.   [3]

Answer

RAM is random access memory, but ROM is read only memory.

RAM is volatile meaning that it is lost when the computer is switched off, but ROM is not.

RAM is used for temporary storage, but ROM is used for permanent storage.

Commentary

*The keyword is **compare**. This means that every sentence you write to score a mark has to contain a comparison, because to get the mark one statement must be compared to another.*

Using the keyword discuss

Question

Discuss the importance of laws for data privacy with reference to the General Data Protection Regulation (GDPR).   [5]

Answer

Digital devices are making it easier to monitor what people are doing. There are CCTV cameras everywhere in towns and cities and communications from phone calls, emails and text messaging can be monitored. Satellites with cameras can see what you are reading or identify a car number plate from space. Many governments are creating databases of DNA and have introduced identity cards and biometric passports.

It is important that laws are passed to protect the individual from these threats to their privacy.

The GDPR is an EU law that is also part of the British Data Protection Act (2018). The GDPR deals with data held about an individual. Some of this is sensitive data, such as racial or ethnic origin, health and religious beliefs.

There are some exceptions to the regulation. These include collection of data for national security, detection of crime and data used privately at home for household or recreational reasons.

By passing the laws and having them enforced, data about ourselves stands less chance of being misused.

Commentary

*The keyword is **discuss**. A discussion means exploring both sides of an argument and explaining statements that you make. Whole sentences must be used. Look at the number of marks – that gives a good indication of the number of points you need to make.*

Read the question carefully and make sure you have answered all parts of it.

1 Problem solving

Some problems are simple, and others are more complex.

Simple problem	Complex problem
Calculate 2 + 2	Calculate the trajectory of a lunar rocket taking into account the wind speed at the launch site.

Decomposition

REVISED

When faced with a complex problem, a computer programmer will break that problem into smaller parts. If those parts are not able to be solved simply, then the parts will be split into separate parts again. This is repeated until solvable units are reached. This is known as **decomposition**.

Abstraction

REVISED

It is not usually possible to deal with problems, such as the lunar rocket problem above, directly using a computer as the problem is too complex. To proceed we must first

- remove unnecessary detail, such as the fact that the 'rocket' is a 'lunar rocket'; it could just be a constant called for example, *lunroc*, which would have weight and dimensions
- simplify the process by giving variable names to things such as wind speed and gravity.

This changing of a humanly expressed problem into one that can be dealt with by a computer is known as **abstraction**.

Figure 2.1.1 Space rocket launch

> **Exam tip**
>
> A computer programmer will usually carry out the process of abstraction before decomposition.

After the complex problem has been simplified, it can be split into **modules**. Each module will be a self-contained part of the program. These modules may be reusable and might be used many times in one program, or be transferred to be incorporated into other programs.

Modules are sometimes called **subroutines** or **functions**.

Modules contain **interfaces** which will allow the value of variables to pass in and out of the modules.

Each module will have to be explained carefully. This explanation is known as **documentation**.

It will be used by other programmers who will later have to maintain the code.

Documentation may contain
- comments within the program
- explanation of variables
- the name of the programmer who wrote the module
- the date when the module was written or version number of the module.

Check your understanding

Match each description on the left to the correct term on the right by drawing a line to link the two.

Description
Notes written by the programmer
Splitting a complex problem into smaller parts
A self-contained subroutine
A way of passing data to a subroutine
Stripping away redundant information

Term
decomposition
abstraction
module
interface
documentation

2 Algorithms and programming constructs

Algorithms

REVISED

An **algorithm**
- is a process or set of rules to be followed in order to produce a solution
- is not language dependent so can be converted into a program in any language
- is an unambiguous specification
- will take an input, process the input and produce an output.

An algorithm can be represented in several forms including
- flowcharts
- pseudocode
- computer programs.

Flowcharts

REVISED

A flowchart allows an algorithm to be represented in a visual way. It is helpful if different shapes are used for different processes when using a flowchart so that the eye can take in, at a glance, what is being represented.

The following flowchart symbols are used in this course.

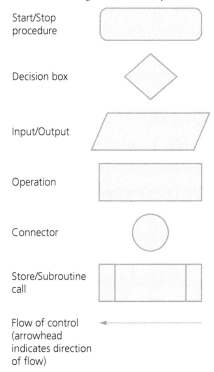

Start/Stop procedure

Decision box

Input/Output

Operation

Connector

Store/Subroutine call

Flow of control (arrowhead indicates direction of flow)

Figure 2.2.1 Flowchart symbols from WJEC Specification (Appendix C)

Pseudocode

When algorithms are written, it is sometimes useful to express the logic of the algorithm without using a specific programming language. Pseudocode is used for this; it gives the idea of the contexts of the program without referring to any special syntax. The rules for pseudocode used in this course are given in the table below.

Construct	Example usage
Declare subroutines	`Declare CapitalLetterOfName` `End Subroutine`
Call a subroutine	`call SubroutineNeeded`
Declare and use arrays	`myarray[99]`
Literal outputs	`output "Please enter a number"`
Variable names	`myvariable`
Define Variable data type	`myvariable is integer`
Data types	`integer, character, string,` `boolean`
Assignment	`set counter = 0`
Selection	`if ... else ... end if`

Indent at least single space after if or do or repeat, etc.	`if counter = 1`
	` output counter`
	`end if`

Annotation	`(Some annotation goes here)`
Comments (Java only)	`/** Comments for Java */`

Repetition	`for i ... next i`
	`repeat ... until`
	`do ... loop`
	`do ... while`
	`while ... repeat`

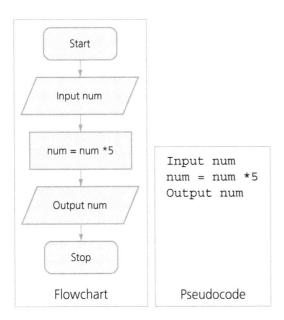

Figure 2.2.2 Comparison of flowchart and pseudocode

Programming constructs

Subroutines

A **subroutine** is a section of code in a program that carries out a specific task that is to be done more than once.

- It can be used many times within a program.
- The code is only written once.
- Values can be sent in and out of subroutines.
- Subroutines are often portable between programs.

Example

A subroutine could perform a validation check on numbers being input into a program.

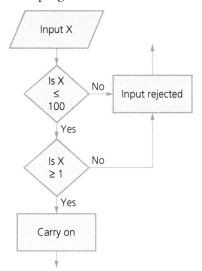

Figure 2.2.3 Flow chart for validation check for numbers between 1 and 100

Each time a number is entered into the program it will be checked by the subroutine above.

Sequence, selection, repetition

Sequence

In a **sequence** of instructions, the instructions are written to be executed in a predetermined order.

Example

```
input number1
input number2
number3 = number1 + number2
output number3
```

Selection

In **selection**, a question is asked and, depending on the answer, the program takes one of two courses of action.

Example

```
input number1
if number1 < 0
   output "Is a negative number"
end if
```

Iteration

An **iteration** is one pass through a process that is repeated. In programming, the sequence of instructions that is being repeated is called a **loop**. Eventually a condition is met, and the loop ends.

At the end of each iteration the result is used to start the next iteration.

There are several types of loops.

The **for** loop repeats a fixed number of times.

Example

```
for i = 1 to 10
  output i
next i
```

A **repeat** loop repeats until a condition at the **end** of the set of instructions is reached.

Example

```
x = 1
repeat
  x = x + 1
until x = 10
```

A **while** loop repeats until a condition at the **beginning** of the set of instructions is reached.

Example

```
x = 10
while x > 1
x = x − 1
output x
```

Counting

REVISED

A **count** variable is used to count how many times an iteration has occurred.

A **rogue value** is a value that falls outside the normal data accepted by the program.

Loops can be terminated
● by counting the number of times the loop has been executed and then stopping at a preselected number of repetitions
● when a rogue value is encountered.

Object-oriented programs

REVISED

In procedural languages, procedures exist independently from the data the procedures use. The data used is separate from the programming code.

Object–oriented languages use **objects** that contain both code and data. This is achieved by

- creating a class which acts as a template for all objects within the class
- objects are created within a class and contain the code and the data required
- the concept of an object containing both the program code and its related data is called 'encapsulation'.

For instance, you could create a class called 'shape', which is a group of objects with similar properties such as colour, number of sides, lengths of sides.

A programmer can define an object in the class of shape and call it 'rectangle'.

A method is an operation on an object within a class that is available to every object within that class. If 'rectangle' has a method for altering its colour, then every shape in the class 'shape' can use that same method to change its colour.

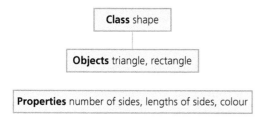

Figure 2.2.4 Relationship between class, objects and properties

A comment is used to explain the purpose of any program code that is written. By inserting comments, the programmer can

- remind themselves what they are doing at that point in the program
- make it readable to other programmers in the future to aid maintenance.

Input, processing and output

REVISED

To have any purpose an algorithm would have to have

- an **input** where for instance a value of a variable was placed into the algorithm
- a **process** where something happens to the input
- an **output** where the result of the processing will be output.

Check your understanding

REVISED

1 Write the terms input, process and output in the correct box.

A $x = 3$	
B $y = x + 5$	
C y	

2 Write down the output from the algorithm in question 1.

y = _____

3 Sketch the flowchart for the algorithm and change the process so that the answer at y is 1.5

Variables

REVISED

A variable is a named storage used in a program that can change its value according to the processes carried out on it.

A variable can be a
- **local variable** that is only recognised within a subroutine
- **global variable** that is recognised and retains its current value throughout all the program instructions including subroutines; it can be called at any time from any subroutine or from the main program.

Identifiers

REVISED

An identifier is a name given to a variable.

Variable identifiers should be meaningful as far as possible. It is better to use the identifier **shapecolour** than the identifier **c**, as **shapecolour** is more meaningful.

Self-documenting code is that which explains itself and saves the programmer having to write too many actual comments to explain what they are doing.

For instance, if we wanted to say that a colour of a shape was red

c = r is not very meaningful

shapecolour = red is much more meaningful and is, therefore, self-documented.

String handling

REVISED

A **string** is a sequence of characters whose order, once defined, is not changed.
- **String passing** is when a string is passed into a subroutine to be operated on.
- **Concatenation** is joining two or more strings together. For example, if string A is Jane and string B is Evans, then the concatenated string is JaneEvans.
- **String comparison** is checking whether two strings reference the same object.
- **Substitution** in object-oriented programming is a principal that if A is a subtype of B, then an object of type B can be replaced by an object of type A.
- **Trimming** is removing leading and trailing spaces from a string.
- **Measuring length** of a string is to find the number of characters in the string.

Mathematical operations

The following mathematical operators are used in computer programming.

Operator	Meaning
>	Greater than
<	Less than
>=	Greater than or equal to
<=	Less than or equal to
<>	Not equal to
==	Equals
+	Plus
-	Minus
/	Divide
*	Times
DIV	Integer division
	Finds the quotient or the 'whole number of times' a divisor can be divided into a number.
	For example, 5 DIV 3 = 1
MOD	Modulo division
	Finds the remainder when a divisor is divided into a number.
	For example, 5 MOD 3 = 2

Logical operations

The following logical operators are used in computer programming.

Operator	Meaning
AND	Both statements must be true for the argument as a whole to be true.
OR	Only one of the statements needs to be true for the argument to be true.
NOT	The opposite of
XOR	The argument is false if both statements are true.
	The argument is false if both statements are false.
	Otherwise the statement is true.

Sorting is arranging data systematically in some sort of order such as
- numerical
- alphabetical.

Data can be in
- ascending order (smallest to largest)
- descending order (largest to smallest).

There are many ways to sort a list, some more efficient than others. Two of those methods are
- **merge sort**
- **bubble sort**.

A merge sort is a **recursive** algorithm, meaning that the subroutine calls itself repeatedly until the list is sorted.

A bubble sort is an **iterative** algorithm, meaning that the process loops repeatedly until the list is sorted.

Merge sort

A merge sort takes the list of items that needs sorting and splits it up into a number of smaller sorted lists.

These lists are then merged together leaving the elements in the correct order.

Example

The list below must be sorted into ascending order.

45	12	23	13	55	3	19	20

First the list is divided in two.

45	12	23	13		55	3	19	20

Each sub-list is divided in two

45	12		23	13		55	3		19	20

until each list is only one element long.

45		12		23		13		55		3		19		20

A merge routine now merges each pair of lists, making sure that the numbers are in ascending order.

12	45		13	23		3	55		19	20

This is repeated

12	13	23	45		3	19	20	55

until the final pair of lists is merged and the elements are all in order.

3	12	13	19	20	23	45	55

Bubble sort

In the bubble sort, the algorithm compares each pair of adjacent items in a list and swaps them if they are in the wrong order. The process is repeated until no swaps are needed.

Example

The list below must be sorted into ascending order.

45	12	23	13	55	3	19	20

The first element in the list is compared to the second element. In this case, 45 is compared to 12. If the first element is larger than the second, they are swapped over.

12	45	23	13	55	3	19	20

The second element is compared to the third. In this case, 45 is greater than 23 and they are swapped over.

12	23	45	13	55	3	19	20

This process is repeated until the last element has been compared.

12	23	13	45	55	3	19	20

12	23	13	45	55	3	19	20
12	23	13	45	3	55	19	20
12	23	13	45	3	19	55	20
12	23	13	45	3	19	20	55

It can be seen that now the largest number (55) is in its correct position.

Starting at the beginning of the list again the process is repeated.

12	23	13	45	3	19	20	55
12	13	23	45	3	19	20	55
12	13	23	45	3	19	20	55
12	13	23	3	45	19	20	55
12	13	23	3	19	45	20	55
12	13	23	3	19	20	45	55

Now the second highest number is in place.

This is repeated until no numbers have changed position at which point the list is sorted.

12	13	23	3	19	20	45	55
12	13	23	3	19	20	45	55
12	13	3	23	19	20	45	55
12	13	3	19	23	20	45	55
12	13	3	19	20	23	45	55

12	13	3	19	20	23	45	55
12	3	13	19	20	23	45	55
12	3	13	19	20	23	45	55
12	3	13	19	20	23	45	55

3	12	13	19	20	23	45	55
3	12	13	19	20	23	45	55
3	12	13	19	20	23	45	55

On the next pass, nothing is changed and so the list is assumed to be in the correct order.

| 3 | 12 | 13 | 19 | 20 | 23 | 45 | 55 |

> **Exam tip**
>
> A merge sort is a recursive algorithm while a bubble sort is an iterative algorithm.

Searching

REVISED

Searching is looking through a list until the item you are looking for is found. This can be done in many ways. Two of the methods for searching a list are
- linear searches
- binary searches.

Linear search

In this simple search, the first item is compared with the item you are looking for.

If that is not the item, then the second item is compared until eventually the item you are looking for is found.

This method can take a long time if the item you are looking for is the last item in the list and the list contains thousands of items.

Binary search

We wish to find the number 12.

First the list must be placed in ascending order.

| 3 | 12 | 13 | 19 | 20 | 23 | 45 | 55 | 70 |

Look at the middle value of the list.

If that value is the one you are looking for, then stop.

If the value you are looking at is bigger than the one you are searching for, then discard the right hand part of the list. Otherwise, discard the left hand part.

20 is bigger than 12 so we discard the right hand side of the list, including 20.

Look at the middle value of the list.

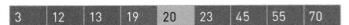

13 is bigger than 12, so we discard the right hand side of the list, including 13. Look at the middle value of the list.

| 3 | 12 |

12 is the number we want, so we stop.

To check whether an algorithm is fit for purpose it should be evaluated and tested.

- **Evaluation** means making an informed judgement about
  - ○ the efficiency of the algorithm
  - ○ whether it meets the original requirements
  - ○ whether it is fit for purpose.
- **Testing** is checking that the algorithm produces the correct results under all circumstances.

To test an algorithm thoroughly test data is used.

The algorithm should be tested using three types of test data

- normal data
- extreme data
- abnormal data.

Example

If an algorithm was created to test that inputs were in a range between 10 and 20 inclusive, we would test using the following data.

Type of test data	Test data	Result expected
Normal	13	13 should be accepted as it is within the given range.
Extreme	10	10 should be expected as it is on the extreme end of the range.
Abnormal	3	3 should be rejected as it is out of the accepted range.

Testing algorithms without using a computer is known as **dry running**.

Dry running often uses a **trace table**.

Example of a dry run using test data and a trace table

This algorithm works out the sum of the positive numbers and the sum of the negative numbers.

Complete the trace table for the following algorithm using the data given.

Test data 3, 5, –1, 6, –5, 9, 0

```
set a = 0
set b = 0
input num
while num <> 0
  if num > 0 a = a + num
  if num < 0 b = b + num
  input num
endwhile
output a
output b
```

num	a	b
3	3	
5	8	
–1	8	–1
6	14	–1
–5	14	–6
9	23	–6

1 A programmer is testing a piece of code that validates an input between 1 and 100 inclusive. The programmer choses three items of test data. Complete the table to show whether the data is normal, extreme or abnormal data.

Data	Type of test data
100	
73	
1	
209	

2 a) Complete the trace table for the algorithm and test data given.
Test data 4, 6, 2, 7, 0

```
set c = 0
set t = 0
set y = 0
input y
while y<>0
  t = t + y
  c = c + 1
  input y
endwhile
output t/c
```

c	t	y	output

b) What is the purpose of this algorithm?

1 a) Add statements to the pseudocode below that will
  i) join strings 'txt' and 'welcome' together
  ii) return the from in 'Hello from Wales'.

```
txt is string
welcome is string
welcome = "Hello from Wales"
txt = "Have a great holiday"
length = len(welcome)
output length
```

b) Write a pseudocode algorithm to find the maximum and minimum of a set of marks.

2 a) Using the notes above to help you, explain using illustrations how a Bubble sort would sort the data below.

8	4	9	3

b) Using the notes above to help you, explain how the binary search would be used to find the number 4 from the list below.

8	4	9	3	8	5	7	3

Answers available online

3 Programming languages

Programming languages are used for writing instructions to be used by a computer.

There are many such languages, each one designed to be useful for a particular purpose.

Hypertext Markup Language (HTML)

HTML
- is the standard language used when writing webpages.
- simplifies the development of webpages and websites.
- enables programmers to read each other's code
- ensures that different web browsers display the page as intended.

Webpages can include
- text
- graphics
- sounds
- video clips
- links.

A web browser, such as Safari or Google Chrome, is used to move around the world wide web from webpage to webpage.

This can be by
- clicking a link
- typing in a particular **universal resource locator** (URL).

An example of a URL is **www.google.co.uk,**

A search engine can be used to locate certain information or particular webpages by typing in the desired word or phrase. The search engine will return the URL of the best fit to your search.

Two examples of search engines are Google and Bing.

The HTML language

The HTML language uses special **tags** which instruct the browser how to display the page. The tags appear in pairs at the start and end of the section to which they refer.

The browser uses the webpage resources to read the HTML tags and build the page, the page is then displayed to the user within the browser window.

> **Exam tip**
>
> HTML uses American spelling; for example, colour is spelt color, and centre is spelt center.

Tags which you will be required to be familiar with are in the table below.

Command	Tag open/close	Explanation
HTML	\<html> \</html>	The start and end of an HTML program
head	\<head> \</head>	Metadata about the code that's invisible to the user
title	\<title> \</title>	Defines a title in the browser tab
body	\<body> \</body>	Holds the main content of a page

Command	Tag open/close	Explanation
img	<img> </img>	Used with the <src> tag allows an image to be embedded within a webpage
headings	<h1> </h1> <h2> </h2>	Defines the type and size of heading depending on the heading type chosen
paragraph	<p> </p>	Denotes a paragraph of text, but often has other tags nested within it such as <img> or <href> Web browsers automatically add space before and after each <p> tag.
italic	<i> </i>	Text within these tags will be italic
bold	<b> </b>	Text within these tags will be bold
centre	<center> </center>	Text within these tags will be centred
list	<ul></ul>	Starts and ends an unordered list
list item	<li></li>	Defines a list item
Hyperlink	<a></a>	Defines a hyperlink

Email address

To show an email address in HTML use **mailto**.

```
<a href = "mailto:Rob@email.com">Send mail to Rob</a>
```

- This creates an email link within the webpage.
- **Send mail to Rob** is the anchor text, which is the text you wish to be displayed on the webpage to represent the link.
- **mailto** is who your email will be sent to.

Hyperlink

To show a link to another webpage use **<a>**

```
<a href="https://www.bbc.co.uk">Visit bbc home</a>
```

The **<a>** tag defines a hyperlink, which is used to link from one page to another.

Example

```
<html>
  <head>
  <title>
Fy ngwefan
  </title>
  </head>
<body>
  <b>My website / Fy ngwefan</b>
  <h2>Holiday pictures</h2>
  <img src = "pwllgwaelodbeach.JPG">
  <p>Holiday at Dinas Island. View of Pwllgwaelod
Beach</p>
</body>
</html>
```

My website / Fy ngwefan

Holiday pictures

Holiday at Dinas Island. View of Pwllgwaelod Beach

Figure 2.3.1 Webpage produced by the code in the previous example.

Assembly language

- Machine code is the language understood by the computer itself – written in binary (0s and 1s).
- Assembly language was created using the structure and instruction set of machine code using mnemonics to make it easier for programmers to remember and understand.

Advantages of assembly language

- Requires less memory and execution time than a high-level language such as C++, Java or Python.
- Allows the code to interact directly with hardware, such as printers.
- Suitable for time-critical processes.

> **Exam tip**
>
> A mnemonic is a pattern of letters that reminds you of something. In assembly language the word used to load the accumulator is LDA.

Assembler Instruction set

Instruction	mnemonic	What does it do?
Input	INP	Inputs a value and stores it in the accumulator
Output	OUT	Displays the contents of the accumulator
Store	STA	Transfers a number from the accumulator to RAM
Load	LDA	Transfers a number from RAM to the accumulator
Add	ADD	Adds the contents of the accumulator to the contents of a RAM address
Subtract	SUB	Subtracts the contents of the accumulator from the contents of a RAM address
Branch	BRA	Jump to the RAM location specified – used for loops
End/Stop/Halt	HLT	Stops the processor
Data definition	DAT	Defines variables

Assembler example

Mnemonic code	Description of action
INP	Input a number
STA Num1	Store the number in a variable Num1
INP	Input a number
STA Num2	Store number in a variable Num2
LDA Num1	Load variable Num1 into the accumulator
ADD Num2	Add the contents of Num2 to the accumulator
OUT	Output the data in the accumulator
HLT	Stop execution of the code

Check your understanding

REVISED

Write assembly code to create the program described on the right of the table.

Mnemonic code	Description of action
	Input a number
	Store the number in Reg1
	Input a number
	Store the number in Reg2
	Load the accumulator with Reg1
	Subtract Reg2
	Output the result
	Stop

Object-oriented programming

Object-oriented programming is a method of programming in a high-level language.

Programming consists of writing code that would logically solve a problem by
- accepting data as an input
- processing the data
- producing an output.

When using an object-oriented approach to programming, the program is written using objects that communicate with each other to solve the problem.

In this course, the platform used to program is called **Greenfoot**. There are several concepts to understand.

Imagine that a program is written about a Spaniel Dog.
- A **world** in Greenfoot is the area in which objects interact. (Where the Spaniel will play.)
- An **object** (the Spaniel) has states (name, colour, breed) and behaviours (barking, running, wagging tail).
- A **class** is a plan or template for creating objects within a program. Here, the class is Dog as there are hundreds of different varieties of Dog.
- Each object is created from a single class, but a class can be used to create many objects.

From the class Dog we can have objects such as Spaniel, BullDog, Labrador, and so on.
- A **method** is used to implement a behaviour.
- One class can contain many methods such as the Spaniel running, Spaniel begging or even Spaniel disappearing.
- **Instance variables** are variables that are bound to class instances.
  - Imagine that you have created a Greenfoot game in which Spaniels move around barking.
  - Each Spaniel will have an instance variable called bark.
  - The bark variable will record how many times each Spaniel has barked.
- **Inheritance** allows a class to use the properties and methods of an existing class. Within Greenfoot, a base class Dog could have a function named wagtail(). The Dog class has a **subclass** named Spaniel and another named BullDog, both of which could implement the wagtail()
- **Encapsulation** is wrapping code and data together into a single unit.

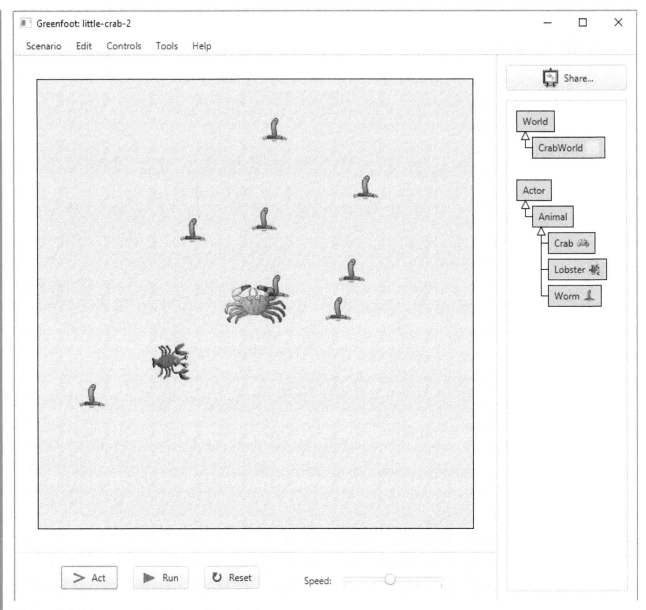

Figure 2.3.2 A screenshot from Greenfoot

The following is an example of what you could be asked to do in the exam in Greenfoot. Tick the boxes when you know how do do each of these things.

What you need to be able to do in Greenfoot	I know this
Create new and extend existing classes and objects.	
Populate a Greenfoot world with objects.	
Create a new Greenfoot world and edit an existing world.	
Write and invoke methods.	
Change existing methods.	
Create new and edit existing properties, including ● public ● private ● static.	
Add and remove objects from worlds.	
Use an actor – an object that has a location in the world and is represented with an icon.	
Move objects around a world. For instance, edit the program code to make the objects move in the direction of the arrow keys when pressed.	
Input from the keyboard.	
Add and play sounds.	
Implement and use parameter passing (by value and by reference).	
Add objects which can receive messages from other objects.	
Access one object from another.	
Implement object collision detection. If a collision occurs, the object is removed.	
Edit objects so that they can turn and move randomly.	
Use the concept of inheritance and encapsulation.	

Now test yourself

TESTED

1 Give the HTML tag needed for each of the following. [3]
Centre text
Insert a title
Insert an email link
2 Write assembler program to add three numbers.

Mnemonic code	Description

3 Explain the following concepts of object-oriented programming.
Class [2]
Object [2]
Method [2]
Inheritance [2]

Answers available online

4 Data structures and data types

Implementing data structures

Data structures were previously covered in Unit 1, Chapter 4.

They include
- one-dimensional and two-dimensional arrays
- files
- records.

Implementing data types

Data types were previously covered in Unit 1, Chapter 4.

They include
- integer
- Boolean
- real
- character
- string.

Variables and constants

A variable is a value in a program that can change.

A constant is a value that remains the same throughout the program.

When a program is written, various **declarations** must be made so that the computer knows how many bits to assign to the variable and the rules by which it can be manipulated.

At the beginning of a program all variables declared will be **global**. Global means that the variables will be recognised throughout the program.

Within a subroutine, it is often useful to have a variable that is only recognised in that subroutine. This kind of variable is declared in the subroutine and is known as a **local** variable.

Variables have **lifetimes**. The lifetime of a variable lasts as long as the program code that uses it.
- Global variables
  - begin to exist when the program starts
  - cease to exist when the program ends.
- Local variables
  - begin to exist when the variable is defined within a subroutine
  - cease to exist when the subroutine ends.

Check your understanding

1 Complete the table by placing the correct item from the list into the correct box
   45.3, TRUE, "Well I never", 3, −3, −4.0, %%^$, +, T, FALSE

integer	real	Boolean	character	string

2 Complete the sentence.

A _____ variable is only recognised in the subroutine in which it has been declared but a _____ variable is recognised throughout the program. This is known as the _____ of the variable.

3 From the algorithm, write down an example of

A declaration	
An array	
A loop	
A real variable	
A comparison	
An assignment	

The purpose of the algorithm is to carry out a binary search for the number X.

The position of X in the array will be given if X exists. If not, then the routine will return −1.

The numbers are already in order and stored in the array **numarray**.

numarray

0	1	2	3	4	...	999
35.0	39.6	40.1	45.1	46.8	...	12345.7

```
numarray[999]
lownum is real
highnum is real
mid is real
set lownum to 0
set highnum to array length - 1
while lownum <= highnum
  set mid to (lownum + highnum) / 2
  if X < numarray[mid] then
      set highnum to mid - 1
  else if X > numarray[mid] then
      set lownum to mid + 1
  else
      return mid
  endif
endwhile
return -1
```

5 Security and authentication

Security techniques

REVISED

The data entering a computer must be accurate, otherwise the results produced will be inaccurate. This is known as GIGO or 'Garbage in – garbage out'. To be as sure as possible that the data being entered into the computer is not garbage the data is

- validated
- verified.

> **Exam tip**
>
> Nothing can check that data is correct.

Methods of both verification and validation have been demonstrated in Unit 1, Chapter 5. Remember, validation checks that data is sensible and follows certain rules, whereas verification checks that the data has been entered correctly.

Validation algorithms

REVISED

Listed below is a subroutine that would only allow valid scores from a test to be input. Each time a number was entered, the subroutine would be called.

```
Declare Subroutine ValidNumber(integer value)
   min is integer
   max is integer
   set min = 0
   set max = 100
   while ((value < min OR value > max))
   do
   output "Please enter a valid number"
   input value
   loop
   return value
End Subroutine
```

It is also useful to make sure that output is sensible.

In the following example, written in JAVA, if the search is successful, a country name and the position of that country in an array is printed. If the search is unsuccessful, the program should report that. We presume that an array of country names (country) already exists.

```
boolean found = false;
int counter = 0;
wantedcountry= JOptionPane.showInputDialog("Please
enter the country that you are looking for");
   do
   {
      if(country[counter] = wantedcountry)
{
   found = true;
   System.out.println("The program found " +
wantedcountry + "at position" + counter + " of the
array");
      {
counter ++
   } while (counter<10 or found = true);
if(found=false)
   {
   System.out.println("The program did not find " +
wantedcountry + " within the array.");
   }
```

Glossary of programming terms

Simplifying the problem

abstraction: changing a human problem into one that can be solved by a computer

decomposition: splitting a complex problem into smaller parts

programming: creating an algorithm in program code

pseudocode: an algorithm not using a specific programming language

Program structure

constant: a value that does not change in the lifetime of the program

documentation: explanation of the program code

function: a subroutine than returns a value

global variable: a variable that is recognised throughout a program

iteration: a process that is repeated

local variable: a variable that is only recognised in a particular subroutine

module: a discrete part of a computer program

repetition: a process that is repeated

selection: following a particular route depending on the answer to a question

sequence: instructions that are written to be executed in a predetermined order

subroutine: a section of program code that can be called many times

variable lifetime: a variable exists only as long as the program code that uses it

Object-oriented programming (OOP)

class: the definition of the method and properties of a group of similar objects

encapsulation: wrapping code and data together into a single unit

inheritance: allows a class to use the properties and methods of an existing class

instance variable: variables that are bound to class instances

method: the behaviour of an object in object-oriented programming

object: a particular instance of a class

object-oriented programming: using objects rather than actions and data rather than logic

Finding errors in the code – debugging

break point: interrupts a program at a specific line

debugging: finding and correcting errors in computer code

error diagnostics: error messages displayed to help the programmer

memory inspector: displays the contents of all the stores in a section of memory

single stepping: executes a program one line at a time when debugging

store dump: displays the contents of all variables used by the program

trace: displays the order in which the program is being executed

variable watch: shows values of variables while program is running